SEASHELL TREASURES
OF THE CARIBBEAN

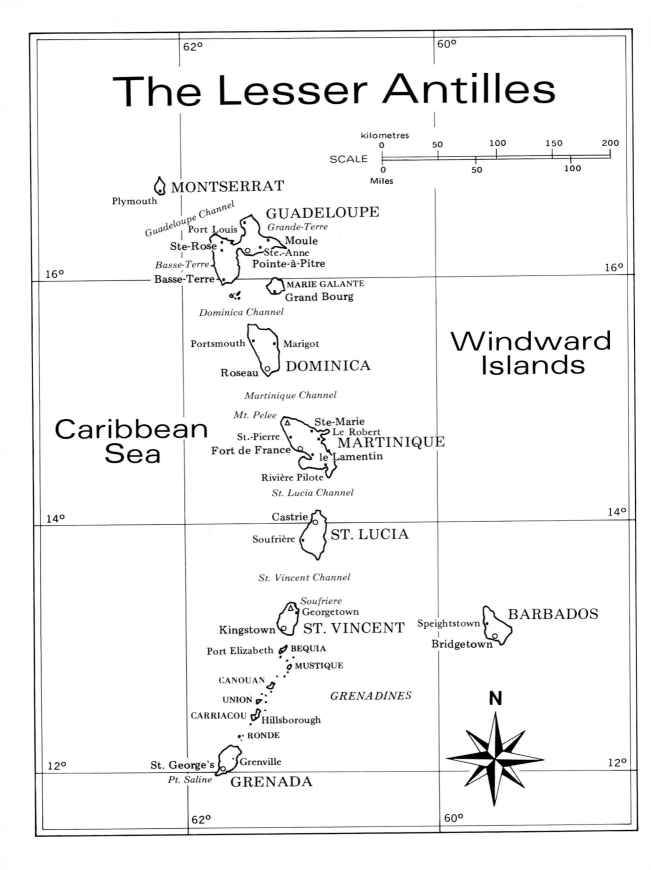

The Lesser Antilles

kilometres
SCALE
Miles

MONTSERRAT

Plymouth

Guadeloupe Channel

GUADELOUPE

Port Louis

Grande-Terre

Moule

Ste-Rose

Ste.-Anne

Basse-Terre

Pointe-à-Pitre

Basse-Terre

MARIE GALANTE

Grand Bourg

Dominica Channel

Portsmouth

Marigot

Windward
Islands

Roseau

DOMINICA

Martinique Channel

Mt. Pelee

Ste-Marie

St.-Pierre

Le Robert

Caribbean
Sea

Fort de France

MARTINIQUE

le Lamentin

Rivière Pilote

St. Lucia Channel

Castrie

ST. LUCIA

Soufrière

St. Vincent Channel

Soufriere

Georgetown

BARBADOS

Kingstown

ST. VINCENT

Speightstown

Port Elizabeth

BEQUIA

Bridgetown

MUSTIQUE

CANOUAN

UNION

GRENADINES

CARRIACOU

Hillsborough

N

RONDE

St. George's

Grenville

Pt. Saline

GRENADA

SEASHELL TREASURES
OF THE CARIBBEAN

LESLEY SUTTY

edited by
R. TUCKER ABBOTT

CARIBBEAN

for Raymond,
these 100 shell treasures
from the Caribbean Sea

Published by Macmillan Caribbean in 1998

Originally published in Singapore under the
title **Cent Coquillages Rares des Antilles.**
Scientific director: Bernard Salvat
Copyright © 1984 by Times Editions
English translation Copyright © 1986 by Times Editions
All rights reserved.

Printed in Malaysia

ISBN: 0-333-74528-0

Contents

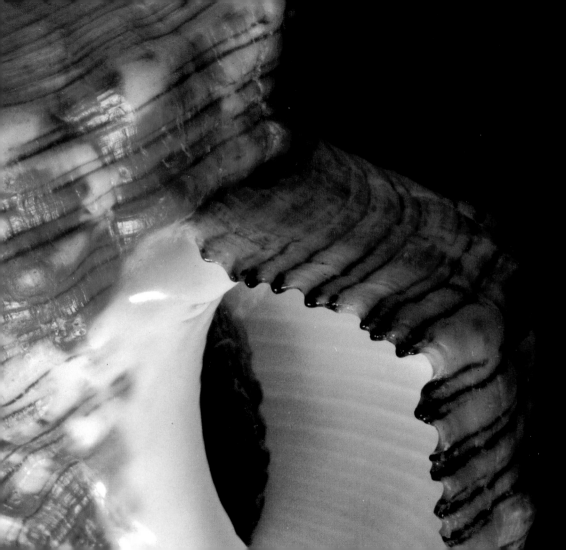

Preface

Unlike most shell books this one has beauty, romance and adventure. It is a splendid example of how a nature lover and ocean enthusiast can delve into the unknown lives of living West Indian mollusks and relay her enthusiasm to us land-locked mortals. Lesley Sutty has roamed and prodded into almost every sea cave and sandy substrate of the Lesser Antilles. Her abilities as a color photographer are exceeded only by the charm of her scientific observations.

Studies such as this can be very important to the scientist, as well as offering inspiration to new students of marine life. For the first time, the colors and shapes of animals and egg masses of many mollusks are recorded. And several long-lost species described more than a hundred years ago have been rediscovered by the intrepid ventures of this talented author.

If you are an amateur conchologist with a yen for collecting, this book will set you afire. If you appreciate beautiful shells, the photographs will seduce you. And if you just plain love shells, the book will entrance you.

R. Tucker Abbott, Ph.D.
American Malacologists, Inc.

Introduction

My longtime quest for the beautiful, elusive mollusk speaks eloquently for the fascination of seashells. Each time I discover a curious and beautiful shell new to my collection I marvel at the amazing ability of these soft-bodied creatures to create such imaginative architecture.

The evolutionary rhythm of life, developed over millions of years, expresses itself in these handsome animals. Yet the exquisite patterns and the intricate houses they build are merely natural responses to nature's need to protect and further develop her many creatures.

The beginnings of this mysterious parade of life are hidden in the millions of years of history of the primeval oceans. The great Tethys Sea of 60 million years ago stretched from the shores of the Americas, across the southern reaches of Europe and thence to the borders of the Indian Ocean. As time isolated and created the Caribbean Sea, the Mediterranean and the seas of the East Indies, so too time created a unique and special sea fauna for the West Indies.

Into this sea garden of beauty, this untouched sanctuary of marine life, came man. First were the aboriginals, Amerindians from Venezuela in the south and Florida in the north, who began to subsist upon the rich resources of these seas. And for perhaps 2,000 years the Arawak and Carib Indians settled and explored the shores of the numerous islands.

It was not until the 16th and 17th centuries that European man came upon the scene and began his exploitations. Although the Spanish, English

1. *The Golden Tulip,* **Pleuroploca gigantea,** *normally from Brazil, has recently been discovered in the Lesser Antilles. (4")*

7

and Dutch were intent upon treasure-hunting for minerals, spices and lumber, their destruction was limited to the land. The coral reefs and sleepy lagoons remained relatively unexplored.

The Caribbean Sea, stretching from the Gulf of Mexico to Brazil, shows peculiar endemic or unique areas within its fauna. As you journey southward, from island to island or bay to bay, you will notice the total absence of certain species or the sudden appearance of one new to you.

In Antigua, small and unique colonies of the Globe Vase, *Vasum globulus*, find shelter among the crevices of the offshore reefs. In St. Barthelemy the Caribbean Vase, *Vasum muricatum*, so rare in Cuba and Florida, will be seen scattered like fallen fruit among the undulating turtle grass of shallow bays. The mossy outer coating, or periostracum, of this uncommon shell blends with the brown and green sea floor. Only an overturned vase shell will sport the vivid mauve of its underside.

Like a few places in Haiti, the beautiful island of Marie Galante in the Lesser Antilles is a haven for flourishing colonies of the Roostertail Conch, *Strombus gallus*, and the Angular Triton, *Cymatium femorale*. The pure, crystalline waters and other environmental conditions are doubtless responsible for their local success. The handsome Golden Tulip shell, *Pleuroploca aurantiaca*, with its strange, blue-starred soft parts, ranges up from Brazil to St. Vincent, but no further north. The stunning cone, *Conus cedonulli*, frequents the archipelago of the Grenadines where it seeks refuge beneath the spines of the poisonous black sea-urchin. Nearby, in deeper waters where currents and dangerous surges sweep through narrow channels, the magnificent Glory-of-the-Atlantic Cone, *Conus granulatus*, may sometimes be found.

I have learned to love and respect the ocean through years of association with the underwater world since early youth, and from my study of the habits and secrets of these strange molluscan creatures.

Who is not moved by the beauty and delicateness of the tiny, fragile wings of the Longhorned Typhis, *Typhis perchardei*, or the unexpected appearance of a Flame Auger, *Terebra taurinus*, lumbering along on the inky bottom in the dim, twilight depths of a Caribbean bay? Or who could remain untouched by the sight of a feathery-mantled Measled Cowrie, *Cypraea zebra*, clinging sullenly to the roof of a somber submarine cave? Look there! See that awkward Carrier Shell, *Xenophora conchyliophora*, lurching forward on the gravelly bottom with its bright scarlet foot extended. And over there, as you glide down with your scuba and fins, is a gathering of small top shells, *Calliostoma euglyptum*, in the depths of a barrel sponge in a pale pink array on the edge of a startling precipice above the deep.

I hope this endeavor of mine to record my experiences in Caribbean conchology will inspire others to study and observe the elusive mollusk. The more we understand them, the more we will be able to protect them for the generations of naturalists to follow.

I have selected 100 specimens to illustrate and comment upon so that the reader may share my enthusiasm and joys in discovering the shells of these beautiful tropical islands. In the last decade I have observed or collected these shells, some rare, others less so, but all exquisite and inspiring.

All the photographs were taken by the author using a "Linhof" camera and a "Nikonos Calypso 11" equipped with a subsea R.2.

2. **Pterynotus phyllopterus**, *the Leafy Winged Murex, is one of the world's most exquisite winged murexes. (3")*

8

1

What is a rare shell?

What is a rare shell?

Seashells which have as their birth places and subsequent habitats areas that are inaccessible and hazardous to man are very often the most enchanting rarities of the molluscan phylum. The star quality of many a mollusk is not dependent upon size. Two obscure rarities are the pale and insignificant Guilding's Lyria, *Lyria guildingi*, the smallest member of the Volutidae family, and the even smaller, quarter-inch long *Arene venustula* of the Trochidae family.

The elusive Glory-of-the-Atlantic Cone, *Conus granulatus*, of slender form and richest golden-red hues, is one of the most coveted of all cone shells and its possession may easily vie in pride with the ownership of its famous South Pacific cousin, *Conus gloriamaris*, of such romantic appeal.

The Leafy-winged Murex, *Pterynotus phyllopterus*, one of the world's most gloriously winged mollusks, lost to conchology for over one and a half centuries, was rediscovered in 1968 off the island of Guadeloupe. It is a breathtaking shell, especially when held in the palm of the hand to observe its extravagance — fragile and perfect, light as a feather, it is a miracle of nature.

The Surinam Cowrie, *Cypraea surinamensis*, stands unique and princely among all the six Cypraeidae of Caribbean waters. It is not only the rarest of the Atlantic cowries, but lives in deep water where most of the specimens so far obtained have come from the stomachs of mollusk-eating fish. Only two

3. *A rare photograph of the equally rare Surinam Cowrie,* **Cypraea surinamensis** *found by the author during a night dive at 50 feet as it was venturing forth from under a maze of sponge and coral. (1.5")*

3.

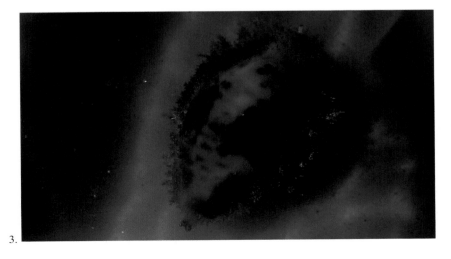

have been live-collected by scuba divers in Florida waters. As few as 50 specimens of this rare cowrie are thought to exist in private and public collections and these are mostly from Brazilian bottom fish.

The two magnificent specimens illustrated on this page came from Martinique, the largest from a 300-foot submarine plateau separating Diamond Rock from the coast of the main island. I recovered one of these from the sea bed — perhaps as a reward after suffering an unfortunate encounter with the stinging tentacles of a *Physalia*, Portuguese-Man-of-War, only minutes before.

The West Indian fauna in many areas has escaped the constant ravages of man, although some edible, shallow-water forms like the Queen, or Pink, Conch have been decimated in a few places. Commercial shelling and dredging has been more intense in the Gulf of Mexico. The precipitous shelves along the borders of West Indian islands have escaped exploitation because of the inaccessibility of the members of this sorely abused phylum.

The shells I talk about in this book, although personally encountered on numerous dives, are mainly hidden from the average human eye amidst the cryptic recesses of offshore reefs and submarine cliffs. Thus, rarity is sometimes a relative term used for specimens yet to be found or collected.

4.

5.

4. *Triton shells,* **Charonia variegata***, are considered molluscan treasures by the native population of the picturesque Grenadine Islands. (8")*

5. *Two specimens of the rare Surinam Cowrie,* **Cypraea surinamensis.** *(1.5")*

6.

Anomalies

There is a fascination among some people for the unusual among the molluscan populations. To some, it is entrancing to find a healthy gastropod beautifully and artistically encumbered with extraneous growths. Sometimes the encrustations of sponges, bryozoans or fire coral, heap up mounds of colorful embellishments that hide the shell underneath.

By far the most outlandish anomaly is the rare individual snail that has forsaken all rules of nature by growing and winding itself in the opposite direction. If it coils dextrally, which is the usual "right-handed" way, its companions and the shell collector accept him without question. But a "left-handed" specimen, coiling in a sinistral direction, can cause confusion among its fellow family members and raise the blood pressure of the

6. *The Queen, or Pink Conch,* **Strombus gigas**, *always beautiful, deeply pink and porcelaneous, is an important source of protein for many West Indian people. (12")*

7. *The Rooster Tail Conch,* **Strombus gallus**, *after repairing the edge of its outer lip. (5")*

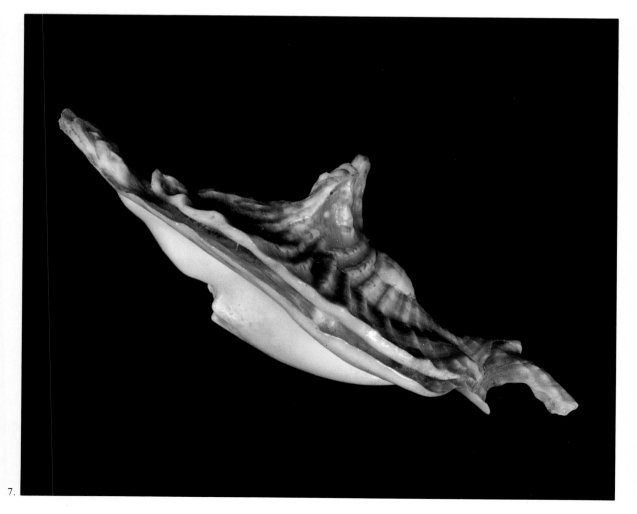

7.

13

lucky shell collector who recognizes and finds it. I have heard of only four or five "left-handed" Queen Conchs, despite the many tens of thousands collected each year. This anomaly is worth its weight in gold.

During my ten years of exploring the waters of the Lesser Antilles I have collected many fascinating anomalies, some of them being magnificent repair jobs to their accidentally broken or twisted shells. A scarred or broken shell, or one with a small hole in the spire, can tell the history of the misfortunes and former battles the mollusk may have fought. Fish, crabs and stormy waters exact a toll on the mollusk and may scar it for life.

Repair work is an essential and curious part of the lives of these soft-bodied animals, and our photograph here shows the perils and providences of a Roostertail Conch, *Strombus gallus*, that I encountered in one of the loveliest of West Indian marine creeks on Terre-de-Bas in the Iles des Saintes, Guadeloupe. Fish and mollusks thrive amidst elkhorn and other corals and sea fans.

Already an unusual pale mauve in color, this *Strombus gallus* had suffered a traumatic experience — a gaping hole incurred dorsally — and this it slowly but surely put to rights. After many months of inactivity, and with determination to reinforce its outside protection to the maximum, it recommenced the task of manufacturing an external housing that would be more foolproof than the first. It is seen that not only has it cemented the badly damaged dorsal area from edge to edge, by a new but somewhat albino conchiolin, but that it has carried repairs many steps further to reinforce the lip. It decided that two are better than one. This is a very exceptional and extraordinary feat of nature. Our hero deserves much praise for so bold a show of common sense.

Anomalies have been with us for millions of years. In fact, some species of fossil cones were normally left-handed, such as the Pliocene sinistral *Conus (Contraconus) adversarius* of southern Florida fossil beds. The species became extinct a few million years later, and today the character of left-handedness in cones is almost unheard of. Only a few Mediterranean ones have been discovered, and only two living specimens in all the Americas.

As for size, mother nature experimented wildly in the Miocene of France. Today our Ceriths are all less than two or three inches in length. In the Paris Basin fossil beds of 30 million years ago, a two-foot monster of a *Cerithium* roamed the ocean bottom. This leviathan outgrew his food supply or served as a food source for some mollusk-eating fish. It was destined to extinction.

I never cease to marvel at the extreme examples of camouflage that nature sports in such vivid colors on the submarine reefs. The brightly mauve-brown and white-striped Turkey Wing, *Arca zebra*, is a gregarious species living in massive colonies in many of the shallow water areas not far from the shores of the leeward coasts of most West Indian islands.

Amused that these wily and well-camouflaged shells gave the game away by rather noisily snapping shut their valves at the approach of danger, I was one day to be dazzled by perhaps the most awesome, yet small, colony of *Arca zebra* so far encountered. Each bivalve was host to a colony of thriving *Millepora* coral which had, depending on the age of both, made life hazardous to say the least for the mollusk. Studying the progressive stages of encroachment by the fire coral it was seen that eventually the polyps were to become responsible for the death of the soft-bodied animal as they invaded the inner side of each valve. The normal filtering movement became seriously impeded and soon the shell could no longer close its valves

8. *Communal living of an unusual nature exists between two startlingly beautiful underwater sea creatures — an uncommon* **Spondylus gussoni** *(2")* *surmounted by an ornate hydrocoral,* **Stylaster rosaceus.**

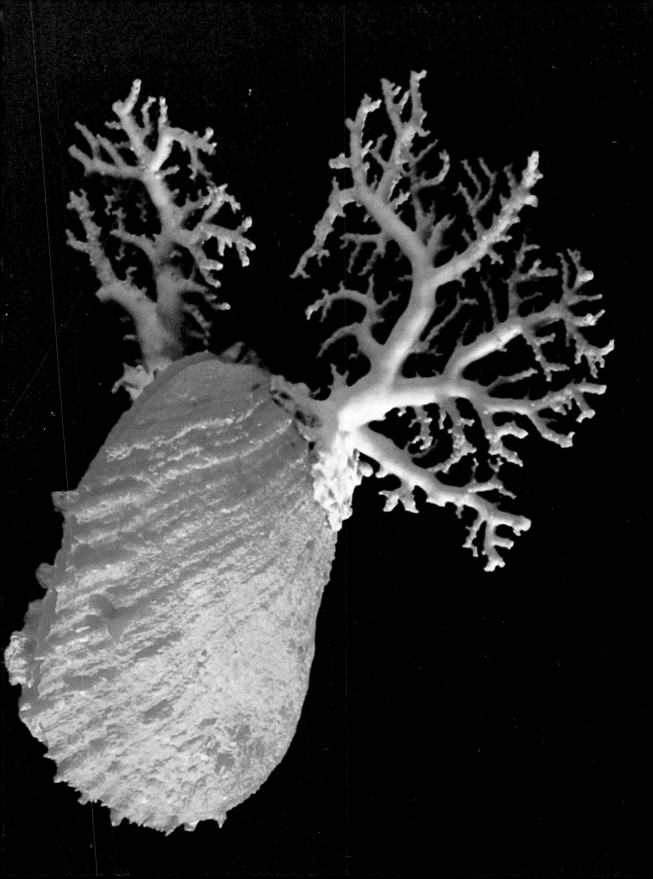

when faced with danger. This was not the only aggression present to make our friends' lives so uncertain; both *Murex brevifrons* and *pomum* were abundant in this same area and deadly predators of the *Arca* both night and day.

One day I discovered a most debonair Thorny Oyster in a cavern of the deep which may claim to be the most beautiful of all anomalies. Exquisite, fragile growths of lilac-colored hydrocoral, *Stylaster rosaceus*, had adopted the magnificent gleaming orange shell of the *Spondylus gussoni* as host; the two had apparently come to an agreement and were living independently of other marine life on the sandy substrate of the grotto.

Nearby I observed a juvenile living in a forest rich in crinoids and parazoa; the lower valve of the shell had built a small but perfect central pedestal of transparent and palest pink conchiolin with which to secure itself to the cliff face.

9. *A heavily encumbered Zebra Ark bivalve,* **Arca zebra***, with an encroaching and ultimately fatal growth of fire coral,* **Millepora.** *(2")*

10. *An astonishing* **Umbraculum umbraculum** *moves slowly across sand and coral rubble in search of algal food. (6") We found it offshore near the volcanic Ile de Ronde, Grenada.*

9.

Strange and beautiful shapes

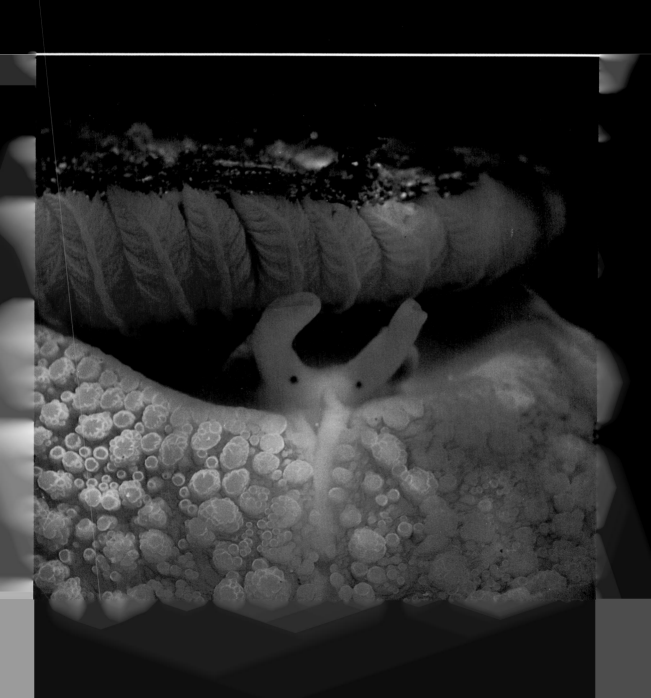

Strange and beautiful shapes

Umbraculum umbraculum
(Lightfoot, 1786)

Atlantic Umbrella Shell

Among the strangest and most startling mollusks to be encountered in the Caribbean Sea is the extraordinary Umbrella Shell, a hermaphrodite whose plump, soft body of saffrons, peach and whites is covered with many, sometimes orange, pimples and protected above by a parasol-like shell — iridescent and yellow and white. A shallow-water dweller, it may be found grazing on the bottom nibbling on sponge, small top shells and ceriths. Few observers realize that this lumbering creature, the size of an orange, is not a sea-cucumber, holothurian or a member of some alien phylum, but is indeed a mollusk. Only when this bizarre animal loses its timidity is the full beauty of its gill plumes, swaying gently above its spaceman body, revealed.

The first mention of this species was made by a British Navy lieutenant in the early 1750's who discovered one alive along the quiet shores of Bermuda. Later, Linnaeus illustrated a similar shell in his 1753 *Museum Tessinianum*, but was so puzzled by it that he called it an operculum. Even Lamarck could not fathom the creature, and called it a hingeless bivalve. In 1767 Abbé Dugast completed a catalogue devoted to "reasoning and systematics of curiosities of nature and art to be found in the Cabinet of Mr Davila"; one of the rarest of these was a "Lepas des Indes" or a Chinese Umbrella.

Some 50 years later, in 1819, Blainville made a trip to London where a friend of this gentleman, Dr Leach, enabled him to discover the organization of the Umbrella Shell, allowing him to dissect a specimen preserved in alcohol at the British Museum. Blainville was somewhat embarrassed by the position the shell should take with regard to the mollusk he studied at the British Museum; upon removal from its jar the preserved animal had the shell firmly adhered to its foot, and despite Lamarck's comment that "this positioning be quite against the rules of nature" Blainville persisted in his belief and went as far as illustrating the Umbrella Shell in an unusual upside-down position in his *Manuel de Malacologie*.

Gaston Moquin-Tandon closely studied numerous Mediterranean species some 40 years later. He was to contribute to a more complete understanding of the *Umbraculum*. Taking to sea each day in a 21-foot sailing launch he dredged the seabed as thoroughly as any man could. His greatest successes were near Chateau d'If, where specimens were collected from between 66 and 132 feet. His 143-page thesis is beautifully illustrated with engravings and dissections.

Caribbean specimens are of a slightly different aspect, in many cases reaching a total length of 7 inches. Their predators are the impressive bottom-feeding rays, sand sharks and puffer fish.

Opisthobranchia
The Nudibranchs or Underwater Seaslugs, butterflies of the molluscan phylum

The most openly colorful, gay and conspicuous branch of the phylum, the nudibranchs, defy collection because their soft bodies resist preservation and rarely possess internal shells. These graceful and exquisite little animals never fail to cause wonder as they glide over sand and rocks at all depths. Delicate scarlet, white and saffron lacey egg masses will be found beneath star and flower corals and even, on one occasion, in a swaying rum bottle trapped beneath the sea's surface in a fish pot some 60 feet down. It housed mother and eggs.

These soft-bodied mollusks may be thought of as the most exquisitely patterned of all marine animals. Many have stinging cells which they harbor within tassel-like projections of their bodies called *cerata*, obtained by feeding on hydroids. This would appear to act as a deterrent in the face of would-be predators.

An unusual case of predation was observed when a small, many-tasseled *Eolis* was collected for identification; the villains were the bright blue wrasses which have the bothersome habit of prying into every corner of the reef where the investigator is located. On this occasion, despite a quick transfer, the sight of the *Eolis* sent the small fish into an extraordinary frenzy, attacking and tearing the container; within seconds the unfortunate seaslug was no longer.

Hexabranchus morsomus
(Marcus and Marcus, 1962)
Swimming Doris

The nudibranchs of the Antilles are numerous, many still in need of identi-fication, and ranging from a sixteenth of an inch to several inches in length. Some appear to live in colonies, others independently, as in the case of the *Hexabranchus morsomus*. A small edition of the Australian *Hexabranchus*

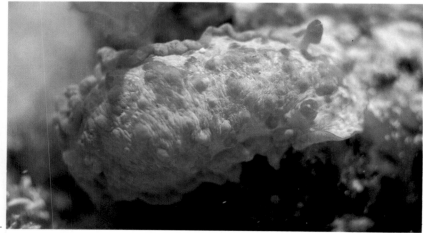

11.

11. *The soft, shell-less nudibranch,* **Hexabranchus morsomus***, varies in color from brightest scarlet to pale pink in order to blend into its marine background. (1.2")*

19

sanguineus, the Caribbean species inhabits both shallow coral reefs and deep offshore waters.

Tom Thompson, a formidable specialist of this fascinating division of the phylum, in a study on *Hexabranchus* described aptly in his introduction the behavior of these gaudy creatures; "the swimming display of *Hexabranchus* is one of the most splendid sights a malacologist may hope for". How true this is, for the little animal considers himself quite the equal of any fish. Gently undulating, gathering momentum and speed, we seem to witness in his movements both warning and an escape motive as the brightly scarlet-edged mantle comes together and apart.

The creatures are hermaphrodites, with both sexes in each individual. Two specimens found cohabiting beneath a small rock covered with red parazoa at 82 feet were placed in the aquarium during the study. Within two hours one was to give birth under the careful and much concerned eye of its suitor. Raising itself into an upright position, literally sitting on its tail, many thousands of eggs then issued from its dilated pouch. The other snail remained faithfully alongside during the two hours needed to deposit the eggs on the corner of an upright "Gaudy Asaphis", a bright mauve bivalve shell. Both animals were more violently colored than at any other time; they remained beside the eggs for nearly 12 hours.

Many members of the molluscan phylum react in this manner. *Coralliophila abbreviata* are observed to release numerous oval capsules which remain adhered to the aperture of the shell when captive.

Glossodoris clenchi
(Russell, 1935)
Neona Blue Doris

Agile and adaptable, the seaslug proves a charming and hardy companion in the aquarium, never failing to surprise. The delightfully flamboyant Blue Doris figured, with its shades of red, turquoise and yellow, gill plumes, tentacles and mantle edges tinged with mauve, resembling a magical harlequin, was encountered carefully choosing a path through a dense population of spiny sea urchins in the shallow waters of an inland reef off the south coast of Martinique. Once in captivity, this half-inch marvel proved the principle animator of the aquarium it was to live in for many months. Constantly busy and inspecting the other occupants in turn, it became particularly attached to a massive *Lima lima*, whose scarlet tentacles aroused its greatest curiosity. *Chromodoris neona* (Marcus, 1955) is a synonym.

Chelidonura hirundinina
(Quoy and Gaimard, 1833)

The *Chelidonura hirundinina* is a little-known tectibranch species of the Caribbean Province. Tropical Western Atlantic specimens are known to exist in the Virgin Islands. In the summer of 1977 specimens were observed in the Grenadines for the first time.

Living in pairs in colonies, these dashing tectibranchs with an internal shell prefer the somber conditions of the deeper waters of ports. Their living quarters may be described as fine sandy hillocks with sparse coral formations. The *Chelidonura* like to position themselves at the summit of these; small holes nearby may or may not be refuges. Another of nature's wonders, with iridescent blues shining brightly on a border of black and darkest orange, with a single white stripe across its back, the lively fellows seen here seem to be taking a step up in order to investigate greener pastures.

12.

13.

12. *Another soft-bodied opisthobranch,* **Chelidonura hirundinina,** *sports a two-pronged tail. (0.5")*

13. *Named after the late Dr William J. Clench, this* **Chromodoris** *surpasses most other members of the reef fauna by its sheer beauty of coloring. (0.35")*

14. *A black* **Murex brevifrons** *dared live among white coralline forests of the Tobago Keys, Grenadines. (3")*

15. *The Emerald Nerite,* **Smaragdia viridis,** *sports the rare green color in both shell and soft parts. It is a favorite among shellcraft hobbyists. (about 0.25")*

14.

15.

Colors

Understanding of the pigmentation and color of the molluscan phylum is a subject fraught with pitfalls. Most scientists will have difficulty in determining the reasons which have caused extreme polymorphism within populations.

Lack of light and unfavorable environment may cause albinism in gastropods and bivalves. Of the spectral colors employed within the molluscan phylum, blue and green are considered the most unusual.

Melanistic species encountered during our study were generally from volcanic substrates. An exception to this rule was the somber black specimen of *Murex brevifrons* that we found on a white coralline substrate. Compared to its fellow members, it was a black sheep of the family. We found our friend not far from mangrove roots bordering the watery channel separating the main islands of the Tobago Keys in the Grenadines. Nearby one may sometimes find other black shells, usually the result of bacteria working on decaying organic matter. The mangrove roots prevent water circulation and further the build-up of hydrogen sulphide. The evil-smelling gas can be responsible for the blackening of dead shells.

Xenophora conchyliophora
(Born, 1780)
The Atlantic Carrier Shell

The Atlantic Carrier Shell, a master in the art of disguise, will from the earliest stages of life accumulate camouflage consisting of bits of pottery, coal, stones, sponges, coral and the shells of other mollusks. Equally at home in the shallower waters of quiet bays and the deeper sand and coral substrate far from shore, its range extends from South Carolina to Brazil.

Only with the onset of somber night will the Carrier Shell become bold. Then a startling scarlet body evolves from within the much-encumbered

16. *An example of the "original conchologist", the Atlantic Carrier Shell,* **Xenophora conchyliophora,** *selects special bivalves or gastropods to glue to itself. (4")*

16.

23

shell. Thus it begins investigations, resembling an incongruous mushroom on a two-inch stalk of boldest red, maneuvering itself and its decorated shell over and around obstacles in search of food and additional bits of debris. These it carefully selects for size and shape; some hours may pass before it has prepared the way for any new addition, which will be quickly adhered to the last whorl — as if by magic.

A very unusual aspect of the *Xenophora* illustrated here is that it has collected both valves of the cockle, *Laevicardium laevigatum*, a bivalve it appears to strongly favor above others.

The rarity of this astonishing gastropod lies in its unique behavior and very creditable imagination with a definite tendency towards self-preservation in a way rarely encountered in the molluscan phylum.

There are two very perfect bivalves ranking among the unusual members of the Caribbean pelecypods whose shape and structure almost defy description. One has splendor, the other simplicity of graceful lines. The Spiny Jewel Box, *Arcinella arcinella* (Linné), may vary from deepest pink and mauve, to delicate yellow and white. The most coveted specimens are those living in deep waters of quiet bays, buried in muddy substrates, at a depth of 66 to 132 feet.

One specimen collected was firmly attached to the columella of a fiery red *Strombus pugilis*; the Jewel Box was purest white and the marriage of the two a stunning sight. The conch must have been seriously impeded by this beautiful parasite, and although they lived for some time in one another's company, it was the *Arcinella* which first succumbed.

Of the 200 species of Ark shells populating tropical seas, the *Anadara chemnitzi* (Philippi), or "Chemnitz's Ark" is one of the most perfect heart-

17. *Like a chestnut burr, the* **Arcinella arcinella** *discourages hungry foragers. It is a common sand-dwelling bivalve offshore. (1.5")*

18. *Graceful beaded riblets adorn the mud-dwelling* **Anadara chemnitzi.** *(1.3") This ark clam is edible.*

17.

18.

24

shaped shells in the phylum. It is a bottom-dweller, showing preference for marine cul-de-sacs; only a groping hand can reveal its presence in the muddy-textured silt. When live, valves are seen to wear a thick periostracum of dark gold; without this the shell is purest white, sometimes with weak pink shadings.

The Ark shell illustrated here is from the Cul-de-Sac of Marin in Martinique.

Patterns

There is an exuberant richness borne by the external housing of a number of the Antillean mollusks that leaves them without equal. The remarkable etchings of the *Conus cedonulli*, the impressive number of variations within the genus *Voluta musica*, the flattering design of *Calliostoma javanicum* and the delicate feathery shadings of the scallop, *Chlamys multisquamata*, are amongst the most striking.

19. *An aberrant, white-banded* **Janthina janthina** *sports an unusual pattern. (1.3")*

20. *The shell of the Tent Olive from the Pacific side of Central America had accidentally been dropped overboard in the West Indies from a visitor's ship. (4")*

21. *The bubble floats keep the* **Janthina** *snails living a pelagic life on the surface of the open ocean. These Purple Sea Snails are often driven ashore after a stormy wind. (1")*

19.

20.

21.

Such external liveries have their reasons — warning, camouflage and in some cases recognition. Cryptic coloration in animal and shell is common, as in the case of cowries that are frequently observed wearing mantles that blend with the parazoa and sponges of deep-water caves they have chosen as homes; seahares and dorids thrive on the fronds of green eel-grass and other algae, changing their outward appearance according to the nature of the weed they consume. Some color patterns would appear to signify adaptability to different environments.

Distinctive patterning is nevertheless a singular disadvantage for the mollusk with regard to its relationship with man, for these are the most coveted of all. The fragile pelagic species, *Janthina janthina*, is to be found in all warm tropical seas, but not with the strange markings of the shell illustrated. Despite an arduous and long journey across oceans and coral reefs, this perfectly formed phenomenon was to find a resting place on the shores of Union Island. The white banding of this *Janthina* and uniformity of color is puzzling. Perhaps it was the work of a parasite causing metabolic disturbances or an irregular bubble float. The apex of the shell in life hangs downward as the snail floats at the surface. It is pale whitish to blend with the white ceiling of the ocean seen by marauding fish from below.

In captivity this gastropod has been seen to lay long, delicate, cigar-shaped egg masses of lavender color to its transparent float. A large specimen of *Janthina globosa* was observed feeding on smaller ones under such conditions.

22. *Swirls, beads and chocolate-colored lines combine to create a conchological masterpiece in these pyramid-shaped* **Calliostoma javanicum.** *(1.5")*

23. *The Matchless Cone of literary fame has incomparable patterns of golden and white patches. (2" to 3")*

22.

3

Treasures of the sea and reef

Treasures of the sea and reef

The following pages represent my personal selection of some one hundred forms of seashells which, when first encountered, afforded the greatest pleasure and most memorable moments of a nine-year association with the Caribbean fauna.

The families treated here have many morphological forms and some are considered great rarities. Innumerable details of the lives of each have been noted and catalogued, all of which is impossible to relate here. Unless otherwise stated, the specimens were collected by me. To the best of my ability I have painted as clear a picture as possible of the fauna of the southern Caribbean.

The regions between Puerto Rico and Trinidad have escaped attention for far too long and the observations made during the study will play only a small part in furthering our knowledge of this poorly known, yet truly fascinating, area of the tropical seas.

Caribbean Cymatiidae

More than one hundred species of *Cymatium* or triton shells are known to exist in the tropical and temperate waters of the globe. Species are widely distributed, which may be accounted for by the lengthy free-swimming stage of the veliger. Those species found in both the Western Atlantic and Indo-Pacific appear to have Tertiary origins and migration would have been aided by the then existing Tethys Sea.

The more colorful and rarer members of this family inhabit deep water, commoner members being found near the littoral and in mangrove swamps. Aggressive carnivores, *Cymatium* have been observed attacking cones and bivalve shells immediately upon starting life in an aquarium. When one or more of these gastropods is present in such conditions, general arguments and squabbling decide who shall have the largest morsel. The senior member usually wins. Freshly collected *Cymatium* from deep waters have been observed to contain *Lima* and small coral crabs intact within the digestive tract. The animals of these attractive shells are usually gloriously colored with leopard-like spots over the entire body.

Charonia variegata
(Lamarck, 1816)
Triton's Trumpet

Thought of as cave dwellers, triton shells also inhabit sandy bottoms, hiding their heads under outcrops of rocks and coral ledges. The most beautiful of these was seen travelling across dense fields of eel-grass 40 feet below the sea's surface, in one of those areas of the Caribbean known to harbor that dubious, glassy-eyed character of the *Sphyraenidae* family, a master of disguise and strength, the barracuda.

One of the richest molluscan havens in the Caribbean is watched over by barracudas. Fearing human invasion, their arrival beside an investigator is immediate. Impressing you by their daring, the circle tightens as they think of you, their imagined prey. Most of these large predators have amused me by their immense curiosity and cunning.

We had travelled by plane, ship, car, and foot to visit the summer breeding grounds of the many mollusks we knew to be present in the area. Within minutes of entering the water, an impressive image appeared, its six feet seeming to emit serious intentions. Although barracuda seldom attack, on this occasion my companion, Philippe Margolis, was attacked from behind when the fish bit his swim fin.

The French surgeon stationed at Marie Galante reported that he had given first aid on several occasions to local fisherman as a result of barracuda attack. Although greedy and daring in their exploits, the barracuda are insatiably curious.

We noted that juvenile triton shells remained closely adhered to the operculum of the mother, sometimes two or three at a time. The length of their stay was not determined. Other specimens were observed under small slabs of coral nearby. The *Charonia variegata* is an extraordinarily predaceous animal, feeding on urchins, tulip and cowrie shells, orphiurans and starfish. It is one of the phylum's most reputable hunters.

Cymatium testudinarium rehderi
(Verrill, 1950)
Rehder's Triton

This is a fairly recently described species. Problems faced with identification may be avoided by noting that the dark glossy inner lip has long parchment-colored plicae which extend across the entire parietal area, a peculiarity absent in other similar *Cymatium*. Reaching a length of four inches, the body whorls bear shades of yellow and orange crossed with white bands. The periostracum is thick; long curly hairs stand out on each of the five or six knobbed axial ridges. The holotype of the species was collected from 25 to 40 fathoms off Dominica in the Lesser Antilles, and is in the

24.

24. *The attractive Goldmouthed Hairy Triton,* **Cymatium nicobaricum,** *has no claim to rarity. It is most abundant in semi-enclosed bays near the shade of mangrove trees. (2")*

29

United States National Museum. The *Cymatium* illustrated here are from deep water south of Dominica where they were collected at a depth of 83 feet in 1972 from sand and coral substrates. Juveniles were observed on shallow reefs of the Grenadines.

The range is thought to be from Cuba to the Lesser Antilles. A small number of specimens are known to have been dredged from deep water by Mr C. John Finlay formerly living in Cuba.

Cymatium krebsi
(Mörch 1877)
Krebs' Hairy Triton

A pale shell, characterized by a glossy, thickly-toothed aperture and thin golden periostracum. This rare *Cymatium* has an extensive range from Palm Beach to Venezuela.

Squat but colorful specimens are occasionally recovered from shrimp trawling nets off Barbados. In Kingstown harbor, St. Vincent, a uniformly chalky white specimen was found tenanted by a hermit crab in company with the turrid, *Polystira albida*, and a *Terebra taurinus*. Adults may reach a length of three inches and are much sought after. No specimens were found at a depth of less than 83 feet. The *Cymatium krebsi* should not be confused with its Eastern Atlantic counterpart *Cymatium corrugatum*.

The holotype is thought to be in the Copenhagen Zoological Museum, where Mörch originally placed it.

Cymatium parthenopeum
(von Salis, 1793)
Giant Hairy Triton

The Giant Hairy Triton is an interesting species with a wide distribution throughout tropical and temperate seas. Workers in the 18th century were disinclined to accept the species as universal and sought to divide this species into several taxa. The original taxon, *Murex parthenopeum*, stems from the ancient city of Parthenope, now modern Naples. Synonyms are *Triton americanum, T. australasiae, T. brasilianum*, to name a few.

Juveniles have been collected in shallow waters of the sublittoral zone off many Caribbean islands. Adults live in deeper waters on the soft muddy bottoms of harbors and bays and such shells may attain six inches or more. Seven pairs of gleaming white teeth adorn the dark brown sculptural folds of the outer lip. The operculum has axial blades and hair-like fringes.

Cymatium femorale
(Linne, 1758)
The Angular Triton

This is one of the few shelled mollusks truly able to boast an impressive and perfectly triangular structure. Admirable in its architecture, richly brown in color, with white-tipped ribs under a velvety and golden periostracum, the Angular Triton will spend most of its life feeding, mating and multi-plying among the glistening, waving clusters of the slender leaves of the eel-grass beds. Here its appetite is well-satisfied by the multitude of small sea creatures lodged within the shoots of these pastures.

25.

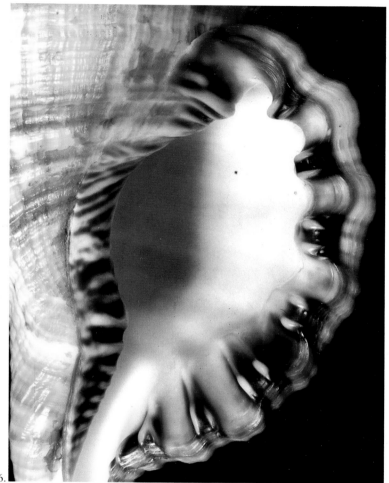

26.

27.

28.

25. *Triton's Trumpet,*
Charonia variegata, *has a*
partridge-like pattern of
soft browns and creams.
This 14" monster
was found off Marie
Galante Island. They feed
on **Linckia** *starfish.*

26. *The Giant Hairy Triton,*
Cymatium parthenopeum, *is*
found in many warm seas
around the world. It is not
very common. (4.5")

27. *The deep-water*
Cymatium krebsi *is hard to*
find but is sometimes trawled
off Barbados and Venezuela
by shrimp fishermen. (3")

28. *Few specimens of the*
copper-colored Rehder's
Triton exist in collections.
This relatively little-known
Cymatium *was discovered off*
Dominica in 1950. (3.5")

31

This *Cymatium* has an inhabitant whose bluish mauve mantle, with its many brown speckles, bears an unrealistically small oval operculum, affording little security or protection for such a grand and gaping aperture. This opening is normally iridescent, but a deep mauve tint may occur in juvenile specimens.

A stoic shallow-water dweller, it is rarely found in deep water where it is observed to be larger and heavier and more typically red in coloring. Specimens have been known to reach more than nine inches in length under such circumstances. Endemic to most of the Caribbean islands, large and isolated colonies are known to exist in Marie Galante and Barbados.

Linatella cingulata
(Lamarck, 1822)
Poulsen's Triton

This unusually beautiful triton shell is endemic to the northern part of the range of the Greater Antilles, living in deep water off the coasts of Florida and Texas. Few specimens have been found south of this area. Two juveniles were salvaged from dredging operations in the Port of Gustavia in St. Barthélemy in 1972. The rich chestnut specimen illustrated here was dredged from deep water in Port-of-Spain, Haiti.

Adult shells may reach three or four inches in length and the elegant spiral cording is covered with a thin, hairy periostracum. The outer lip is crenellated with the pattern of the body whorl reflected on the inner side of the pale aperture. Lamarck first described this species in 1816 as *Fusus cutaceus* in his third volume of *Tableau Encyclopedique et Methodique*; since this time the original shell has disappeared from view. A more recent synonym is *Linatella poulsenii* Mörch.

Distorsio constricta macgintyi
(Emerson and Puffer, 1953)
McGinty's Distorsio

A surprising species, the McGinty's Distorsio is the rarest of the three Western Atlantic *Distorsio*. Distorted and gnarled, the beautiful dark orange parietal shield is covered with heavy white pustules, while the body whorls are pale yellow or white, unevenly knobbly, with a fine furry straw-colored periostracum. An adult shell measures just under two inches.

The specimen illustrated here is from a depth of 132 feet on fine substrates; a large *Charonia variegata* was its companion. Somber channel conditions are often adopted as a dwelling place by this species; other *Distorsio* were detected in shallow water off the leeward coasts of St. Vincent and Grenada in estuarine conditions.

First mention of this mollusk is attributed to Dall who, in 1889, made light of this species in the Bulletin of the Museum of Comparative Zoology; he believed it was merely a variety of the common *Distorsio clathrata* (Lamarck, 1822). Three species closely resembling each other live in the Caribbean — *D. perdistorta, D. clathrata* and *D. constricta macgintyi*. Hal Lewis of Philadelphia, Pennsylvania, wrote an excellent research article on this complex in *The Nautilus* journal in 1982 (vol 86, pp. 27—50).

29. *The Angular Triton,* **Cymatium femorale,** *possesses an oriental charm, preferring to live among eel-grass beds. The aperture of young specimens is a delicate mauve. (4")*

29.

30.

31.

30. **Linatella cingulata** *is one of the more unique members of the triton family. It is rare in the West Indies but common off the east coast of Mexico. (2")*

31. *One of the most naturally deformed of all the marine shells is McGinty's Distorsio, rare in the Caribbean but not uncommon off the east coast of Florida. (3.6")*

Bursa thomae
(Orbigny, 1842)
St. Thomas Frog Shell

This species has a delicately bluish mauve-colored animal with yellow spots and prune-tipped, swaying tentacles, protruding from its cumbersome housing. Outside the shell is a covering of marine growth closely matching the purple glazing of the aperture.

The St. Thomas Frog shell is an uncommon and beautiful species of *Bursa* which lives hidden within rocky crevices. Breeding takes place during the early spring and late summer months. The animal will often choose an empty bivalve to house the hundreds of tightly packed violet-colored eggs which are laid in a layer of circular form, corresponding to the aperture of the mother; these she will smother as if to keep her brood from harm.

Found throughout the Caribbean province, this attractive gastropod inhabits shallow offshore waters and sand and coral substrates as deep as 132 feet. The largest specimen observed during the study measured two inches; most full grown adults reach little more than an inch in length.

Bursa corrugata
(Perry, 1811)
Gaudy Frog Shell

It is not usual to find this attractive species in any part of the Antillean range; most known specimens come from the coast of Central America. More recently the Gaudy Frog Shell has been found in deep water on sand and coral bottoms off Marie Galante and Martinique. Humfrey, in his 1975 study on Jamaican shells, mentions their presence in several bays of Jamaica under rocks at a depth of 10 to 90 feet, which corresponds with the specimens found south of this region.

Young specimens have fine fragile outer lips, with a transparent cast and silvery sheen. The inside of the aperture in fresh specimens is tinted with mauve. The varices are golden with white denticles on each. The body whorls are yellow-gold with many beadings between the strong nodules.

Adults have been observed to reach a length of three inches. In these, the former lips are of a sturdier matter, much thickened and deep orange; the outer lip bears pairs of strong teeth, all a gerontic sign of age.

Arene venustula
(Aguayo and Rehder, 1936)
Venuste Arene

Rarest of the tiny members of the genus *Arene* (pronounced "a-reen-ee"), this is a deep-water dweller. Here its range was extended from Florida and Puerto Rico to the south of Martinique where a specimen was collected in 1972 at a depth of 100 feet on a sand and coral seascape.

The shell measures one quarter of an inch, and possesses four body whorls decorated with a series of revolving triangular spines, beneath which are deeply channeled ribs, separating the shell into tiers. The overall color of the shell is fawn. The pearly aperture bears an unusual operculum which is multi-spiral and deeply hollow, bearing a central pinprick of black. The deep umbilicus is fringed by numerous spines.

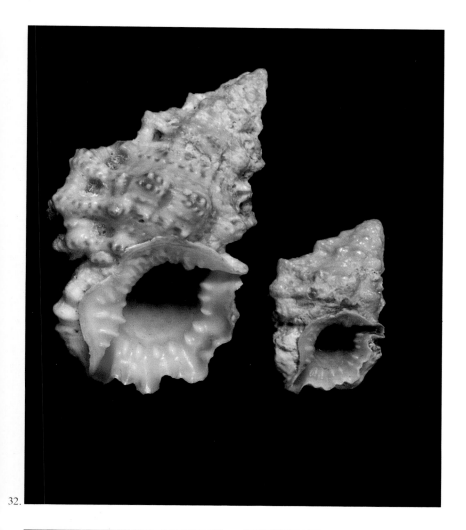

32.

33.

34.

32. *The St. Thomas Frog Shell displays a delicate, violet, glossy aperture. (1.4")* The male shells are usually the smaller.

33 and 34. *The Gaudy Frog Shell when young has a fragile outer lip, but when mature it thickens and bears white teeth. (1.5")*

Turbo canaliculatus
(Hermann, 1781)
Channeled Turban

A rare turban varying from rich chestnut to olive-green with darker maculations over the body whorls. Deep, smooth channels divide the shell into four parts; a thick, shelly, operculum protects the animal from predators.

This handsomest of gastropods has been observed in relative abundance in one small area of its range off the northern coast of Guadeloupe in the French West Indies where the Atlantic joins the Caribbean Sea. Creole fishermen reap the harvest of the sea by placing fish pots on the sea bed at depths from 25 to 200 feet; currents are strong. These conditions, where substrates are mostly sand with few coral formations, seem to suit the Channeled Turban. It is rare for a live specimen to penetrate and lose itself within the prison of the traps. Instead, our crustacean friend the hermit crab will do so, having taken over this elegant house. A symbiotic relationship would seem to exist between the crab and adherent sea anemones. The anemone offers protection perhaps with his stinging tentacles, recovering at the same time morsels of food not consumed by the crab.

A live specimen was collected from the intertidal zone of the Grand Cul-de-Sac of St. Barthelemy in 1969. Beachworn specimens were found on Union Island. In most areas in the Caribbean it is quite uncommon.

Calliostoma euglyptum
(A. Adams, 1854)
Sculptured Top Shell

These palest pink, delicate top shells have a range far wider than imagined. Considered rare southeast of Florida, where it favors moderately shallow water, *Calliostoma euglyptum* colonizes depths which would account for its rarity. Marine cliffs of Dominica house, within the darkness of deep barrel sponges, numerous specimens of the gregarious, sponge-eating Sculptured Top Shell. Revealing a fondness for crowds, as many as 42 of these bright, nacreous little shells have been observed to share the same vast living quarters; not to their advantage one would think, but serenely squashed up into a few square inches, piled one upon the other, they may congregate to enjoy a common feeding ground.

The animal is uniformly white with two light-brown specks for visual organs. Shells rarely reach more than three-quarters of an inch in length.

Calliostoma javanicum
(Gmelin, 1791)
Chocolate-lined Top Shell

There are few more enchanting encounters to be experienced than that of meeting this gentle and vivacious top shell as it glides smoothly across the undersurface of madrepores, retracting immediately at the threat of disturbance. Fragile tentacles swaying and its mantle a perfect imitation of the shell it carries, black streamers on glorious golden yellow, this creature is surely one of the most aesthetic of all marine mollusks.

It is a crevice-dweller, rarely seen active other than at night. A deep-water species reaching two inches in diameter, *Calliostoma javanicum* may be very frequently found throughout its range from 15 to 100 feet.

35.

36.

37.

35 and 36. *The coveted Channeled Turban lives in small communities off the coast of Guadeloupe. (3") The operculum is white, smooth and shelly.*

37. *The rare Venuste Arene was found for the first time in Martinique in 1972, thus extending its range far to the south of Florida. (0.35")*

38.

39.

Calliostoma jeanneae
(Clench and Turner, 1960)

An extremely rare *Calliostoma* was dredged by the *Atlantis*, an American research vessel, off Havana, Cuba, and described as a new species, *Calliostoma jeanneae*, as recently as 1960 by Clench and Turner in *Johnsonia*, volume 4, no. 40. The range and specimens examined were known only from the type locality. It resembled no other Atlantic *Calliostoma*.

In 1973, in a small bay to the north of Fort-de-France in Martinique, hermit crabs were discovered bearing upon their shoulders no less gems than this same iridescent, pink-hued beauty. *Calliostoma jeanneae* is thought to be a deep-water species, and it is possible that the crabs had carried these rare little shells inland. Mlle Jeanine Dhuicq, a devotee to the cause of conchology in the Caribbean, reported finding other specimens from the littoral zone not far distant from this same area.

Calliostoma pulchrum
(C. B. Adams, 1850)
Beautiful Top Shell

Charles B. Adams was to find the original specimen of the diminutive and delicately sculptured *Calliostoma pulchrum* in Jamaica during his second field trip there in 1848. Devoted to the smaller shells of the West Indian fauna, he made descriptions that were colorful and evocative. The microscopic details of the numerous small and delicate gastropod were not to escape his attention.

He described the Beautiful Top Shell, an uncommon member of that genus, in terms that retain the charm of a bygone century. He informs us that this species was "conical, much elevated; pale claret color, with a dark brown apex, and large ill-defined spots of white"; after a lengthy analysis of the structure he continues: "a subtruncate columella, a subquadrate aperture" concluding almost in disappointment "umbilicus wanting" and, finally, of the angle of the spire he wrote: "mean divergence 48°". His hundreds of descriptions of conchological structure were to prove incomparable.

The holotype is in the Museum of Comparative Zoology at Harvard University; its range is extensive, from Florida to the coast of Brazil.

Epitonium albidum
(Orbigny, 1842)
Bladed Wentletrap

Most of the evocative and delicately sculptured Staircase Shells from Caribbean waters rarely attain more than an inch in length. Wentletraps are predators, hungrily feeding on the roots of colorful sea anemones, adapting themselves to life at most depths. *Epitoniidae* tend to adopt the color of the food that nourishes them. The spire of the Wentletrap has inspired artists and architects; thus the spiral staircase is a constant reminder of the symmetry and design of the axial rotation of the bladed body whorls.

Epitonium albidum, illustrated here, are indeed giants from the deep. From sand and coral rubble at a depth of 66 to 132 feet in Martinique and St. Lucia, specimens measured twice that of a normal adult.

40.

38. *Pearly tracings decorate the shiny whorls of the small* **Calliostoma jeanneae.** *(0.25")*

39. *A "herd" of the lovely Sculptured Top Shell,* **Calliostoma euglyptum.** *(0.75")*

40. *The Chocolate-lined Top Shell,* **Calliostoma javanicum.** *(1.5")*

41. *Beauty hides on the underside of* **Calliostoma pulchrum** *collected first in 1848 in Jamaica by Charles B. Adams. (0.25")*

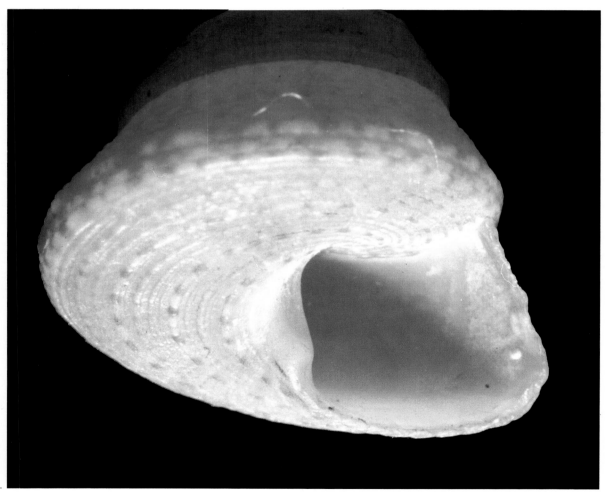

41.

Turritella exoleta
(Linné 1758)
Eastern Turret Shell

A pale *Turritella exoleta* makes slow progress through the fine sand at the base of a marine cliff; usually these slender shells are pale fawn; ciliary feeders, they will spend most of their lives hidden in the soft strata beneath the coral, *Agaricia fragilis*. This exquisite shell is moderately common in certain islands of the West Indies and seemingly absent in others.

Perfect specimens are a rarity, as the fragile lamellae decorating the whorls are easily damaged. A small circular operculum offers protection for the animal which will retract deep within when the snail is alarmed.

Strombus gallus
(Linné, 1758)
Rooster Tail Conch

Rarest of the five West Indian conchs, *Strombus gallus* is known to gather during the summer months in order to breed. This is an intriguing sight; they assemble themselves into groups of twos, fours and sixes. Days later the process of laying long, thin gelatinous egg strands begins.

The older a specimen, the longer its "rooster" tail. The largest collected during the study came from the bottom of a marine cliff in Martinique at a depth of 115 feet. The uninhabited shell was ochre-colored, measuring a length of seven and a half inches — a world-record size according to Wagner and Abbott's "Standard Catalog of Shells".

Rooster Tail conchs sport brilliant colors, varying from pink to scarlet, purple, mahogany, orange, yellow and occasionally albino. All of these morphological variants are to be found within the same community. Lips may be more or less widely flared, at times crenellated and edged with green. Juveniles have lacy, tailless transparent lips and are even more brilliantly colored.

Strombus gallus appear to favor the central part of the range and are less frequently encountered in the south. As with all Strombidae, the Rooster Tail Conch possesses a muscular foot capable of hoisting the shell off the bottom and allowing it to hop along at quite some speed. The sickle-shaped operculum serves as an efficient pole-vaulter for this active herbivore.

Cypraea mus
(Linné, 1758)
The Mouse Cowrie

One of the oddest of the southern Caribbean cowrie shells is *Cyprea mus* which has a limited range extending no further north than Grenada. Here shells have been found off the southern coast off Fort Jeudy in eel-grass.

This species is considered geologically old, resembling fossil species living many million years ago. Bearing superficial similarities to the rare *Cypraea fultoni* and *teulerei*, the richly speckled Mouse Cowrie may be separated from the former two by the dark stains on the base.

In all cowrie shells the mantle extends over the entire surface in order to protect, repair and maintain the glossy surface. *Cypraea* are careful to choose well-secured coral and rock formations as hiding places.

April and September have been observed as breeding times for many

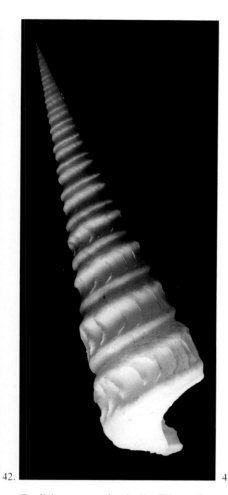

42.

43.

Caribbean cowrie shells. They will be seen in small groups brooding on the eggs. Alas, octopi are greedy predators at such times, sensing the abundance of the *Cypraea*. Morning observations of the *Octopus vulgaris* nocturnal activities were saddening and disastrous; snowy white egg masses of the *Cypraea cinerea* Gmelin were now unattended. Before the octopus' den lay 23 unhappily empty shells of this cowrie. Affection for the very intelligent octopus was provisionally diminished. It was a compelling task to continue observation of this onslaught, as I was unable to rescue the breeding cowries. Within a period of ten days only two percent of the brooding animals had escaped this cephalopod doom.

Stigmaulax sulcata
(Born, 1778)

Sulcate Natica

A member of the family Naticidae, this three-quarters-of-an-inch treasure is the only known member of the genus *Stigmaulax* in the tropical Western Atlantic. The variation of the species with strong cancellate sculpturing is known as *Stigmaulax sulcata* forma *cancellatus* Hermann 1781.

42. *A shell with many scaly whorls — the Eastern Turret Shell,* **Turritella exoleta.** *(3")*

43. *Few shells can boast of such exquisite translucency as the deep-water wentletraps,* **Epitoniidae.** *(1.5")*

43

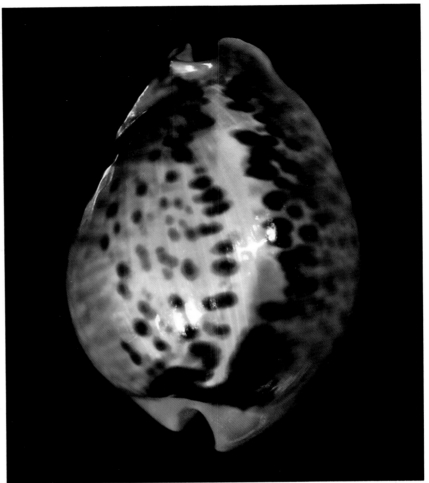

44.

44. *The Mouse Cowrie,*
Cypraea mus, *inhabits
the coastal waters
of Venezuela. (1.7")*

45. *The Rooster Tail Conch,*
Strombus gallus, *has a
flaring tail. The color of the
shell can be yellow to mauve
or brown. (6")*

46. *A female Gray Atlantic
Cowrie (1.3") broods over her
eggs. The octopus is
particularly fond of cowries.
It drills a hole in the shell
and injects a poison.*

45.

This member of the family is coveted by those collectors wishing to have a complete set of these colorful West Indian snails. The axial ribbing is an outstanding feature found in no other member of the family. The operculum is calcareous with one thick central rib.

It is a deep-water species scattered throughout the Antilles from Florida to Brazil. Specimens have been found in association with colonies of *Cassis tuberosa* on sandy bottoms near channels separating islands. Boring holes into, and feeding voraciously on other small mollusks, the *Stigmaulax* spends its daylight hours buried beneath the soft, yellow sand of its habitat.

Cassis flammea
(Linné, 1758)
Princess Helmet

As early as 1685 the Flame Helmet was reported from the shores of Jamaica by Queen Anne's physician, Martin Lister. French naturalists in 1792 reported it abundant along the coast of Martinique and Guadeloupe.

Contrary to common belief these handsome gastropods may reach the size of an adult *Cassis tuberosa* when left to live in the quiet seclusion of the seaweed beds of enclosed bays and marine cul-de-sacs; these may attain seven inches when adult. Smaller specimens are observed to favor the shallow waters of inshore coral reefs where they will remain buried in the sand during daylight hours.

It is common in the Bahamas but uncommon in the southern Caribbean. Only a handful of these beautiful shells, with their glossy, lynx-like patterns, were collected during our four years of observations between St. Vincent and Grenada. Many specimens still exist in bays and coves of Guadeloupe, Marie Galante, the Saints and Martinique.

Cassis tuberosa
(Linné, 1758)
King Helmet Shell

Certainly the most loved, ancient and sought-after of the larger West Indian gastropods, the King Helmet shell may be encountered infrequently throughout its Antillean range.

Early sailors who first found this species on trips to Hispaniola must have been stunned by the handsome serpent-like dorsal pattern and rich coloring. The unexpected array of toothy protrusions on either side of the inner lip, displayed on an expanse of shimmering creamy porcelain, would explain the avidity with which this shelled animal has been collected over the last 2000 years by Amerindians and ardent modern conchologists. The former would marinate the rather bitter-tasting flesh of the mollusk in herbs and seeds, then carefully chip out the inner whorls and face of the shell to provide a cup or recipient of solid matter. In Europe the Italians and French developed the fine art of cameo cutting. There is today a noticeable reduction of populations.

Dependent upon the lowly pincushion-like sea urchin for nourishment, the helmet shell will, when deprived of this food, move to new areas where it is likely to find other beds of echinoderms. The massive muscular foot will smother the urchin; the mollusk then spends some hours ingesting and digesting its prey. Then, as is its custom, it will burrow into the sand with perhaps only the main dorsal spine indicating its presence. The creature is

47.

47. Stigmaulax sulcata, *a rare moon snail with a shelly operculum prefers deep channel waters. (0.75")*

48. *The Flame Helmet secretes with its soft fleshy mantle many beautiful pleats of creamy calcium carbonate crystals. (5")*

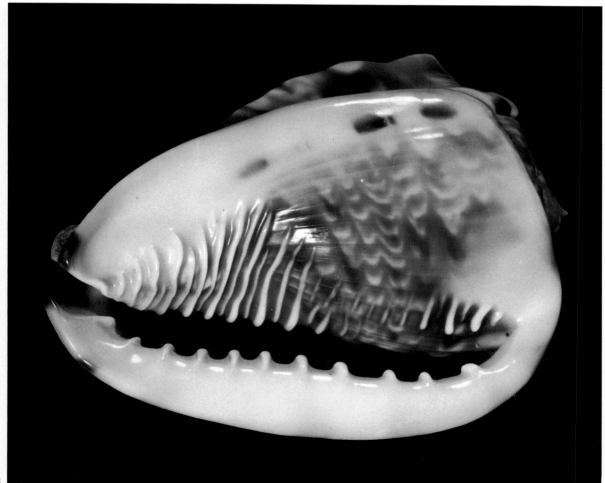

48.

capable of completing this amazing disappearing act within a few seconds.

Helmet shells appreciate the clearer waters of channels where fairly strong east-west currents are predominant. A 20-year-old specimen may attain a length of 12 inches and be covered with thick calcareous concretions. One of Nature's helpers, protecting the coral reef from the often destructive urchin, this remarkable mollusk deserves respect and consideration all too often lacking.

Cassis madagascariensis
(Lamarck, 1822)
Emperor Helmet Shell

Handsomest of the Caribbean *Cassis*, with its splendid flame-colored lip, this giant is found more frequently in the Greater Antilles where it prefers deep water. In the southern Caribbean it may be considered a rarity. Single shells have been observed travelling across floors of sandy bays in the Grenadines, Martinique and Grenada. An exceptionally large specimen measuring 13½" and weighing some four pounds was collected by Mrs Carty from Sandy Ground, Anguilla.

The most interesting observations were made in the channel between Antigua and Guadeloupe; here a small but handsome colony of this large gastropod was detected. Detection here is no mild description, for swimming against strong currents and swells of the Atlantic meeting the Caribbean is arduous. In what appeared to be dunes of yellow sand, 100 feet below the surface of this chaos, were sparse marine growths and the rare rose-colored echinoderm, *Plagiobrissus grandis*. Many of these appeared to have served as a meal for some hungry *Cassis* passerby. Our interest was drawn to undulating strands of red algae. The weed had attached itself to the main dorsal spine of the helmet shell, the only indication of the shell's presence deep in the sand; this proved to be a consistent clue.

Lamarck, in his description of the shell in *Animaux sans vertebres*, gave the locality as Madagascar. This was an error, but the original name has had to be retained according to the rules of nomenclature.

Muricidae

A varied family of ever-hungry carnivorous beauties, more than 400 known species of Muricidae exist in tropical and temperate waters; some of the rarest are from the Caribbean. In volume I of *Johnsonia* of 1945, W. J. Clench and I. Perez Farfante were to unravel many of the intricacies of the Western Atlantic murexes, correcting the confusing earlier works of well-meaning conchologists.

Melbourne Carriker carried out a fascinating study in 1972 on the removal of spines by muricids during shell growth (volume 15, no. 2 of *The Veliger*). We are told how the murex grows, hibernates and dissolves unwanted spines that will hinder further extension of the next body whorl. Some shells were observed completing this operation within eight or ten days. The parietal area is cleaned, spines removed at the base by the mantle by chemical dissolution; secretion of the new intervarix shell and spine then commences. Many of the murexes are known to be dye-giving; *Murex pomum* secretes perhaps the most effective of all; it is an odiferous substance that is probably distasteful to predators.

49. *The King Helmet,* **Cassis tuberosa,** *is a greedy consumer of spiny sea urchins. The shell is over-collected and disappearing near tourist-traveled islands. (7")*

50. *The Emperor Helmets congregate in deep water and burrow into the sand. Sometimes only a sprig of red algae growing on the highest spine will reveal their presence beneath the surface. (8")*

51. *The amber-colored* **Pinna carnea** *often falls victim to a hungry Murex or octopus in the area. (7")*

Pterynotus phyllopterus

(Lamarck, 1822)

Leafy-winged Murex

In January 1969, at the beginning of this survey on the rarer Caribbean seashells, an astonishingly beautiful species of *Pterynotus* was discovered off the northwest coast of the island of Guadeloupe at a depth of 66 feet amid sand and coral. Embellished by three exquisitely fluted deep orange wings, the shell appeared to be an undescribed West Indian species.

Other stations were established between Guadeloupe and Martinique over a period of 18 months; the mollusk proved to be endemic but rare. Some specimens bore a strong resemblance to the *Murex rubridentatus* Reeve 1846, at present in the Hugh Cuming collection at the British Museum of Natural History and that figured by Sowerby in his *Thesaurus Conchyliorum*. Sowerby was unaware of the habitat.

In December of 1969 Dr John Taylor of the Department of Molluscs of the British Museum advised further research, and in September of the following year, when live specimens were collected at a depth of 40 feet, it was finally possible to identify this murex.

There was a magnificent paratype of Lamarck's *Murex phyllopterus* engraved in color in Volume III of Louis Kiener's *Species general et iconographie des coquilles vivantes: Genre Rocher* published in 1842–1843; the shell, a treasured possession of Lamarck's, was thought to originate from the Indian Ocean. The true habitat had been wrongly transcribed during the voyage home when in fact it must have come from the "West Indian Seas". Ships in those days were returning home laden with many hitherto unknown species; such an error could easily have been made.

The shell behaves in a manner expected of a rock species, hiding in small but deep hollows of rock or madrepore. It is unusual for this *Pterynotus* to stray far from its dwelling place.

The anatomy — hitherto unknown — of this rare murex is typical of the genus. The radula or "teeth" of the animal consist of three navicular-shaped cusps of diminishing sizes, superimposed one upon the other, hinged together at their base; the edges are microscopically serrated, the whole reminiscent of a flowering tulip cut in half. The animal is cream-colored with minute red dots; the tentacles are long and finely spotted; black specks represent the visual organs, the verge is darkly bordered with mauve. The aperture of the shell has six to nine denticles which may be pink, red or unicolored depending on diet. The base color varies from shades of peach and orange to vermilion and musk, but rarely albino. Adult shells may attain a length of three-and-a-quarter inches.

Perfect specimens are very uncommon and are mostly seen in museum collections. The Museum of Natural History in Paris possesses one of the finest. Several private shell collectors in America and Europe have now purchased lovely examples.

52. The famed Leafy-winged Murex, **Pterynotus phyllopterus,** *was lost to science for 150 years. The lower, darker specimen was the first to be rediscovered by the author off the coast of Guadeloupe in January 1969. (2.5")*

Murex spectrum

(Reeve, 1846)

Spectral Murex

This is one of the most exquisitely colored of the rare West Indian murex shells, and is a close relative to the equally stunning *Murex palmarosae* from Sri Lanka in the Indian Ocean. Dark brown or charcoal adorns the

many spines which decorate each varix of the golden or bright red body whorls. Most specimens collected alive are coated with such a dense layer of foreign matter that they are scarcely recognizable as treasures.

Living in both shallow and deep water not too far from the coast, they bury themselves in fine sand near rocks and madrepores. Only at night as it goes in search of prey will the animal unfold itself from within to reveal a glowing yellow body.

The holotype of *Murex spectrum* was mentioned by Sowerby in his *Thesaurus Conchyliorum* published in 1879 and consequently renamed *Murex argo* by Clench and Farfante in 1945. Abbott in *American Seashells* (1974) retained Reeve's original name proposed in 1846.

This shell comes from Jamaica and the Greater Antilles while specimens were collected alive in both Grenada and Martinique during our study. This is a large murex reaching at least six inches when adult. Senile members of this species were collected in three feet of water, while the young have been found at a depth of 100 feet, these being the most colorful, with fragile flaring lips unlike that of the fully grown shell, which bears a small, circular, closed aperture.

Murex beauii
(Fischer and Bernardi, 1857)
Beau's Murex

This most coveted deep-water murex shell was first collected by Commander Beau of the French navy off Marie Galante in 1857; it was described at great length in the fifth volume of the *Journal de Conchyliologie* of that year.

Specimens dredged from 100 to 200 fathoms have beautifully webbed varices; throughout the Antillean range this is a very unusual sight. Two shallow-water *Murex beauii* were encountered at 40 feet on mud substrates of a marine cul-de-sac in Martinique, where visibility was at its lowest. The largest of the two was moribund with its operculum resting nearby. A little distance away rock formations served as homes for numerous oyster shells which provided food for this carnivorous murex.

Murex cailleti
(Petit, 1856)
Caillet's Murex

Caillet's Murex is an uncommon deepwater species usually dredged from between 50 and 200 fathoms. This angular murex shell may also be found at a depth of 66 to 115 feet at the bottom of marine cliffs, hidden beneath small rock and coral formations in soft, mud substrates. Distinguished from others by the finer, more numerous intervarical ridges, the shell is sturdy and plump. Pinkish brown or yellow with paler background, adult specimens may reach two-and-a-half inches in length.

A specimen in the aquarium proved to be as hostile as the rest of the mingling marine fauna. Considering a nearby Pen Shell, it advanced towards it with devious intentions, leaning itself against one side of the upright and unsuspecting bivalve, finally inserting its proboscis between the slightly gaping valves, which snapped shut at this invasion. After a series of six or seven such attacks the *Pinna* keeled over on its side, burdened by the weight of the predator.

53. French Commander Beau collected the original **Murex beauii** *from deep water off the island of Marie Galante, in 1857. (5 ")*

54. **Murex spectrum** *hides its reds and golds beneath thick layers of encrustations of algae, sponge and bryozoans. The soft parts are colored a pale ochre. (5 ")*

55 and 56. Small murexes, such as the uncommon **Murex cailleti,** *are voracious feeders on clams and other snails. (2.5")*

53.

54.

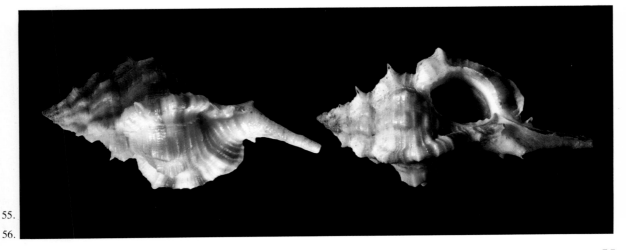

55.

56.

Murex consuelae
(A. H. Verrill, 1950)

Consuela's Murex

Endemic to the Virgin Islands and the Lesser Antilles, the *Murex consuelae*, until recently known as *Murex pulcher* (A. Adams), bears few of the typical murex characteristics. Possessing hardly noticeable blunt spines and few matrix decorations, the slender body whorls may be seen to have small delicately webbed varices. The siphonal canal is sharply recurved; two-and-a-half inches is the maximum length for this pink and ochre-colored shell.

The animal spends its days slightly buried in sand pockets at the base of marine cliffs. A group of ten *Murex consuelae* were observed breeding in deep water in a cave at Layou, St. Vincent, where they had congregated during the month of February 1971.

Murex pomum
(Gmelin, 1791)

Apple Murex

This is a common, but distinctly colored, murex thought originally to have come from West African waters, but soon known to later explorers as a typical West Indian species. The brown spot in the upper section of the inner lip identifies this species.

Usually inhabiting shallow inshore waters, *Murex pomum* was collected from sand and coral ground at a depth of 66 feet off the west coast of Guadeloupe. Such finely fluted and brightly colored specimens are infrequently encountered.

57.

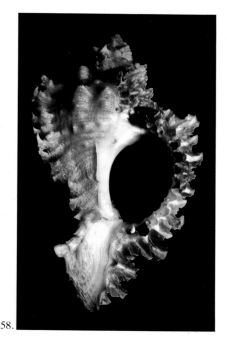

58.

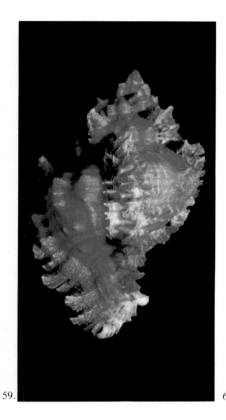

59.

60.

The largest specimen collected was from Terre de Haut in the Saintes, measuring six inches and cunningly installed beneath a pier where fish and conch were cleaned daily. It had obviously enjoyed a well-fed and peaceful existence.

Hexaplex strausi
(Verrill, 1950)
Straus' Murex

I am told by Dr R. Tucker Abbott, a co-author of *Caribbean Seashells*, that this is one of the most exciting finds in many years. The naturalist A. Hyatt Verrill was reporting and describing many strange shells from the Caribbean 35 years ago. Most of them were dead examples of Pacific species brought by travellers to the West Indies. Although much of Verrill's work is considered erroneous (this is not the Yale scientist, Addison Verrill, 1839–1927), one or two of his new species have turned out to be valid.

Hexaplex strausi is an example. It does live in the Lesser Antilles, as I found two living specimens in Martinique. The first one, an inch and a half in length, was discovered near a fish trap in 21 feet of water. It was busily consuming a small tellin clam. After a lengthy and excited search I found its companion crawling on the wooden trap. Verrill found adults and young specimens off Dominica Island, reportedly in 75 to 100 fathoms of water. It is an unforgettable thrill to rediscover a "lost" species.

57. *A rare, rediscovered murex,* **Hexaplex strausi,** *had not been found for 30 years since Verrill described it from the Antilles. We found them near wooden fish traps. (1.3")*

58 *and* 59. *The Apple Murex is fairly common and found off South Carolina to Brazil. Specimens in deeper water have scarlet apertures. (3")*

60. *Consuela's Murex, once known as* **Murex pulcher,** *favors life in sand pockets near marine cliffs. (2.5")*

Ocenebra (Risomurex) rosea
(Reeve, 1856)
Pink Drupe

In the southern Caribbean, deep in the roots of burning fire coral of an offshore reef, a small community of brightly colored *Risomurex* was encountered. Standing out at a distance, despite their small size, they cunningly placed themselves in cracks covered with nematocysts from the corals, providing sure protection from the many reef predators.

A similar *Risomurex* was found in deep water living on rocks and coral off Diamond Rock in Martinique. Both specimens measured half an inch and bore a series of seven heavy nodules with overall orange coloring. Those of the Grenadines were less nodulose, finely fimbriated, with a series of dark brown revolving beads on the body whorls. In both gastropods the aperture bore five strong teeth. The columella bore a deep notch and two white plicae. The horny sickle-shaped operculum entirely fills the deep fuschia-colored opening, and is firmly held in place by the solid white denticles. The animal is brownish orange. Rios features a similar specimen in his *Coastal Brazilian Seashells* as *Morula necocheana* (Pilsbry).

Talityphis perchardei
(Radwin & D'Attilio, 1976)
Percharde's Typhis

This charming and delicate, inch-long jewel is one of the great rarities of the Caribbean. It was discovered and described less than ten years ago, and the name honors Peter Percharde, a fisheries officer in Trinidad. The species is sometimes dredged in 50 to 100 fathoms in Martinique and off Surinam. It was originally discovered off Bocas, Trinidad, but we found it on the Atlantic side of St. Lucia where it seeks shelter in silt in the deep.

The small, tubelike projections, probably used to draw in fresh seawater, are typical of the muricid subfamily, Typhinae. The glassy sheen in the shell of this species is almost a pure white, although some specimens may be orange- or rosy-tinted, especially at the tips of the tubes and the siphon.

Genus *Coralliophila*
(H. and A. Adams, 1853)

Four species of coral shells are known to exist in the Caribbean, two of which are uncommon and rarely found live. Delicately sculptured, the two members to be discussed seem to avoid collection of heavy encrustations so frequently encountered on the shallow-water *Coralliophila caribaea* and *abbreviata* which live in large colonies on most of the known reef corals.

Coralliophila aberrans
(C. B. Adams, 1850)
Globular Coral Shell

Measuring from half an inch to one inch the rare Globular Coral Shell shows preference for the deeper waters, nesting in small, inaccessible hollows. Two specimens were observed feeding on the base of a sea anemone in 90 feet of water at Diamond Rock off Martinique. The animals appeared to have enjoyed an undisturbed life judging by their unusual size.

The light gray foot bears a wine-hued operculum. The small specimen

61. *When not nestled near a protective seafan,* **Coralliophila abbreviata,** *may become covered with calcareous growths. (1")*

62. *The brilliant* **Risomurex** *is a small jewel found among the colorful coral reefs. (1.3")*

63. *Glassy horns decorate the fragile whorls of the rare, inch-long Percharde's Typhis. (1")*

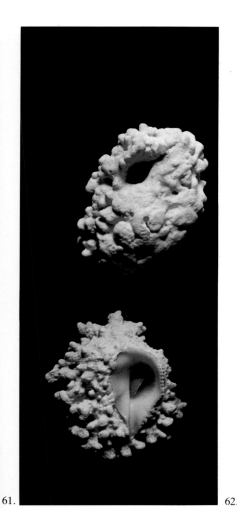

61.

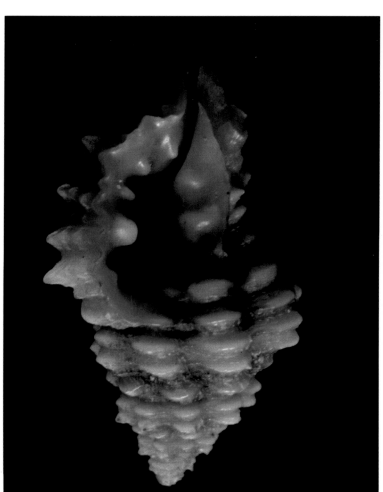

62.

63.

illustrated here was found in shallower water browsing on the roots of gorgonians. The association of *Coralliophila* with the pale pink rods may have been coincidence, whereas little doubt remains as to the preference of the other members of this group. Once in the aquarium and in company of the anemone, *Condylactis gigantea*, the coral shells nourished themselves from the organic matter at the base of the anemone.

C. B. Adams described this species from Jamaica during his field trip there in 1848—1849, and Humphrey, during his recent studies of Jamaican fauna in 1975, described specimens from under rocks in shallow water. This habitat closely resembles that of the allied Mediterranean *Coralliophila*. This shell extends from the Gulf of Mexico to the Lesser Antilles.

Coralliophila scalariformis
(Lamarck, 1822)
Ladder Coral Shell

As with *Coralliophila abberans*, the *Coralliophila scalariformis* is thought to be lacking a radula. In all cases, live specimens of the unusual Ladder Coral Shell were collected from crevices of the starlet coral, *Siderastrea siderea* and the lettuce coral, *Agaricia agaricites*.

This very angulate shell, bearing spines on the body whorl, has a cherry-red operculum to enhance the aperture. The siphonal canal is stained with orange, the only highlight of an otherwise uniformly white shell and animal. I have collected this lovely shell in Guadeloupe, Martinique and the Grenadines from marine cliffs in some 60 feet of water. The range extends from Florida to the Lesser Antilles.

Latirus infundibulum
(Gmelin, 1791)
Brown-lined Latirus

Favoring shallow muddy substrates, the elegant Brown-lined Latirus can be observed on rare occasions in deep offshore waters where they tend to paleness as in the smaller illustrated specimen. These will be found buried in soft sand at the base of marine cliffs under small blocks of *Madrepora*.

The larger specimen, measuring three-and-a-half inches, is from eelgrass and shallow water. It sported a thick velvety periostracum absent in the deepwater *Latirus infundibulum*. The umbilicus in this aged gastropod had taken on extraordinary proportions to a breadth of one half an inch. It is an exceedingly handsome shell with its numerous spiral cords and strong axial ribs; the animal is scarlet with white spots.

Rare in the northern part of the range, its main distributional areas would seem to be the islands of the Lesser Antilles.

Latirus cariniferus macgintyi
(Pilsbry, 1939)
Macginty's Latirus

This rare form of the West Indian *Latirus cariniferus* (Lamarck, 1822) with its golden shades, keeled body whorls and somewhat open umbilical chink, is very close to the more typical form. Both forms attain a length of two-and-a-half inches and may live together. The form *macgintyi* lacks the brown axial bars between the ribs.

64. Wavy, frilly spiral ribs decorate the white shell of **Coralliophila aberrans** *whose soft parts are also white. (1")*

65. Latirus shells produce delicate, funnel-shaped egg-capsules, in this case filled with strawberry-colored eggs. (0.15")

66. Reminiscent of an oriental shrine, the aptly-named Pagoda Coral Shell inhabits the deep waters off the Antilles. (1")

60

64.

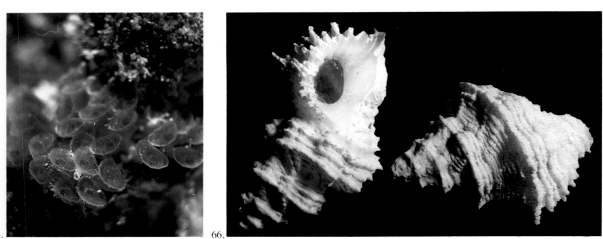

65.

66.

This is a polymorphic species, inclined to environmental change, living in both deep and shallow waters from two to 100 fathoms; fossil records are mostly known from the Pliocene.

The specimens illustrated are from Port-au-Prince, Haiti, where they were dredged from muddy bottoms at 30 fathoms. Further south of this area records of the shells presence are scarce.

Latirus species
(cf. *attenuatus* (Reeve, 1847))

This small *Latirus* bears a distinct resemblance to the *Latirus virginensis* Abbott, 1958 and, better still, *L. attenuatus* (Reeve, 1847).

Collected live in 1970 from Deshaies Harbor in Guadeloupe, the aperture of the shell is deep purple; measuring an inch, both animal and shell clung to the roof of a small dark grotto; its companion was the largest green moray eel yet seen, which flaunted its six feet of muscles as dissuasion of any further investigation of his obscurity. Both inhabited a massive castle-like block of *Porites* coral at a depth of 20 feet. The upper crust housed giant crayfish and spider crabs — all in all, a treasure trove.

The shell has seven body whorls decorated with eight strong white nodules, with dark stains between each of these. The last whorl is plain and those of the umbilicus are shiny white. No other such specimens were collected in the area during the entire study.

67 and 68. The golden colored McGinty's Latirus is a strange variation. These came from off Port-au-Prince, Haiti. (2 ins.)

69. Two variations of the common Brown-lined Latirus. The one in the foreground is 3.5" in length.

67.

68.

Fusinus nobilis
(Reeve, 1848)
Noble Spindle

The two spindle shells shown here in figure 72 are from Barbados where they were found on fine sand and broken coral substrates at 30 fathoms. Their presence was revealed by the strange tractor-tread marks of hermit crabs which had taken these specimens as houses. A mystery surrounds these specimens, since it is believed that they represent relatively young individuals of the huge, eight-inch long-lost *Fusinus nobilis* Reeve.

Characteristic of many *Fusinus*, the Noble Spindle starts off life with many whorls with strong axial ribs. The last whorl lacks this rib. Had our specimens lived for another year or two would their last whorls have been without the ribs? Not until another scuba diver finds one will we know.

George W. Tryon, the Philadelphia conchologist, wrote 103 years ago in Volume III of his *Manual of Conchology*, "the specimen figured is the only one known; a shell sent to me by a London dealer under this name [*nobilis*] came from the island of Tortola, British West Indies."

Do we have strange variations of a well-known species, an immature specimen of the rare *F. nobilis*, or a new species? Only more collecting and intensive study by a competent, professional malacologist will solve this intriguing and exciting mystery of the Caribbean depths.

Fusinus closter
(Philippi, 1850)

This beautiful member of the genus was hauled from 100 fathoms off the coast of Venezuela by a shrimp trawler in 1974.

The specimen illustrated in figure 71 is a perfection of nature at her best; the golden sheen of the eight body whorls is accentuated on the last whorl as the fine axial ribbing takes a graceful downward sweep upon meeting the slender siphonal canal. Elongated palest yellow beads cut the shell into two parts. The lirate oval aperture is suffused with lighter banding; this rare *Fusinus* is considered to be of Brazilian and Venezuelan origin.

Pleuroploca aurantiaca
(Lamarck, 1816)
Golden Tulip

A meeting with the blue-star-spangled *Pleuroploca aurantiaca*, a rare cousin to the banded Tulip Shell, was to be the prelude to an extraordinary journey through luxuriant growths of peacock-hued gorgonias, golden and pink seawhips and dark orange corals.

It had been finally possible to anchor off the Catholic Bank to the west of Mayero Island, where sea conditions are bad and extensive underwater study far from easy. On a sandy desert, 45 feet beneath the ocean's surface, the brightly scarlet *Pleuroploca* ventured forth from the dark crevice of an isolated madrepore. It had a thick sickle-shaped operculum and purest white aperture with many glistening ribs which were bordered with pairs of darkest brown teeth.

Known only from Brazil to date, this beautiful gastropod would appear to be equally at home in the southern Caribbean islands as far north as St. Vincent. It is a deep-water dweller, favoring zones where currents are strong, waters clear and the fauna generally rich.

70. *This delicate mauve Latirus, only an inch in length, was found inside a small cave.*

71. *Few shells may claim the simple elegance of this variation of* **Fusinus closter** *from Venezuela. (3")*

72. *Two handsome spindle shells (2.8" and 3.5") are from Barbados. We believe these are young* **Fusinus nobilis** *Reeve.*

70.

71.

72.

65

73.

74.

Oliva porphyria
(Linné, 1758)

The Tent Olive of Panama

Beautiful shells are carried all around the world by tourists and amateur conchologists. Accidentally they are sometimes tossed aside or lost overboard from a boat. The money cowrie of the South Seas has been found in English waters; the Venus Comb Murex of the Philippines has been found on a New England beach, and many large California abalones were once scattered on the reefs near Santiago, Cuba, after a shipwreck.

A shimmering and wealthy relative to the less colorful Caribbean olive shells, the Tent Olive from the Gulf of California has a kaleidoscope of intricate graphic markings and eye-assaulting arrays of small tents. With its exceptional size of some four to six inches, the *Oliva porphyria* may be considered as one of the most coveted of living jewels.

Preferring the warmer, turbid offshore waters, this highly carnivorous mollusk may be observed in all its glory, displaying an equally exotic mantle. These gorgeous olive shells may be found off the Panamanian coast on the Pacific side. The stray specimen illustrated here comes from the port of Point-a-Pitre, Guadeloupe. Doubtlessly it was a castaway rescued by a local hermit crab.

Ancilla tankervillii
(Swainson, 1825)

Tankerville's Ancilla

One of the most eye-catching members of the phylum, the brightly golden *Ancilla tankervillei* is uncommon in all parts of its range. Favoring the Venezuelan coastal islands it may be observed on sand and coral substrates at a depth of 16 to 33 feet.

It has a massive, muscular foot and mantle of white with black maculations. This enfolds over the entire shell, thus affording it total protection. Tankerville's Ancilla may be separated from the *A. glabrata* (Linné, 1758) in that the former bears a strong tooth on the upper part of the outer apertural lip. The operculum is transparent, horny and pale yellow.

This species is often found in company with other members of the Olividae family. The largest specimen collected was three inches in length, while most adult specimens measured about one-and-a-half inches.

Vasum capitellum
(Linné, 1758)

Spiny Caribbean Vase

Living in muddy conditions, *Vasum capitellum* will rarely be found in the perfect condition of the specimens shown on page 70. Rare in the Greater Antilles, the Spiny Caribbean Vase is abundant in certain areas south of Guadeloupe.

Feeding on bivalves and worms, a pair of magnificent albino *Vasum capitellum* were recovered from a depth of 66 feet in the pass of the Grand Cul-de-Sac of Guadeloupe. Both were outsize, measuring three inches. The animals of both of these small shells were albino with transparent, horn-colored operculums.

The shell is usually cream with a bright-orange aperture; the animal is orange-speckled with fawn; the operculum is thick and almost black.

73. *These glossy* **Ancilla tankervillii** *are great rarities from the north coast of South America. (2.5")*

74. *The exquisite Tent Olive comes from the Pacific side of Central America. A shell collector dropped it overboard in the Lesser Antilles. (4")*

75. **Pleuroploca aurantiaca** *found from the Lesser Antilles to Brazil has a blue- star-spangled animal and brown horny operculum. (5")*

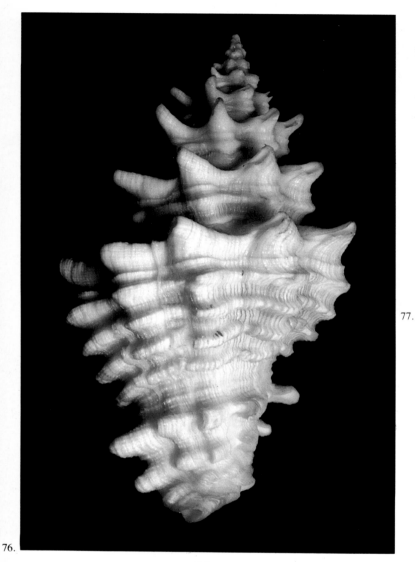

77.

76 and 77. *The Spiny Vase
of the Caribbean is a
handsome catch, but the
white one on the left
is an almost unheard
of treasure. (4")*

78. *Normally having
handsome rounded axial ribs,*
Vasum globulus, *in this case
has hidden its fine
sculpturing with calcareous
growths. The aperture is pink
in fresh specimens. (1.2")*

76.

Vasum globulus
(Lamarck, 1816)

subspecies *nuttingi* (Henderson, 1919)
Globe Vase

Strangest of the West Indian Vase Shells, *Vasum globulus* would appear to prefer life among the corals. One unique and very small colony has been observed living among *Acropora palmata* or Elkhorn coral off the west coast of Antigua. Occasionally, nearer shore on reef flats, one may find them in good condition in Falmouth Harbour.

Abbott created the special subgenus, *Globivasum*, for this unique Globe Vase which reaches only one inch in size. Young specimens of little more than half an inch will have delicate flaring lips.

Volutidae

This is a handsome family poorly represented in Caribbean waters by only three members of the genus *Voluta* and some 20 members of other sub-families. All of these may be considered scarce and much sought after. Aggressive, carnivorous, enfolding their prey in their soft foot for later consumption, the exotic patterns and rich colors of animal and shell are responsible for some of the most gratifying observations.

Dall informs us that the Western Atlantic Volutidae were to first make their appearance in the Cretaceous; little change has taken place since. Mostly tropical in distribution, they may occur from intertidal regions to the deepest parts of the ocean. Some genera, such as *Amoria* and *Scaphella* from elsewhere, do not have an operculum.

Voluta ebraea
(Linné, 1758)
Hebrew Volute

The volute is far from lethargic in its activity. The unexpected appearance from beneath a living forest of Elkhorn coral heads of the much encumbered Hebrew Volute, towards its sandy living quarters beyond, was more than spectacular. Held captive in its foot was a navy blue *Pusio* snail. The Miniature Triton Trumpet's hopes of escape were slim indeed. The color-fully maculated mollusk continued its journey with renewed vigor, devoting its trailing foot to towing away the dismally injured *Pusio*.

This unusual appearance of the Hebrew Volute in the Grenadine Islands would in many ways point to migration in a northerly direction of a species we have thought of until now as a typically Brazilian seashell. The range may now be considered to extend from Brazil to the southern Caribbean, including St. Vincent. Of the three shells collected, two were live and measured three to five inches.

Voluta musica
(Linné, 1758)
Music Volute

The famous Music Volute is typically southern Caribbean, being compara-tively rare or absent elsewhere. It reaches a length of four inches on occa-sions. The color may vary from orange to gray-blue on a paler background. The animal seeks its food in bright sunlight as well as on nightly forages.

Seemingly affected by its environment and food the volute may sport other unusual colorings: two such specimens are shown and are of so unusual an aspect that some would fall into the embarrassing trap of suggesting a new species. This was to be the pitfall of many 19th century conchologists who, confused by the considerable number of variations in shell morphology, were to be responsible for as many as 16 synonyms of this species.

The lavishly painted red volute is from deep water off the south coast of Martinique; the exquisite luster of the paler volute owes its existence to the white sands of the Testigos islands of Venezuela. *Voluta musica* place their eggs in capsules, often inside dead bivalve shells. As many as three or four capsules with two or three minute but perfect volutes in each may be placed in the protective inside of a dead valve of a *Glycymeris* or *Codakia*.

79. *The Brazilian Hebrew Volute has recently been found as far north as the Grenadine Islands. (4")*

79

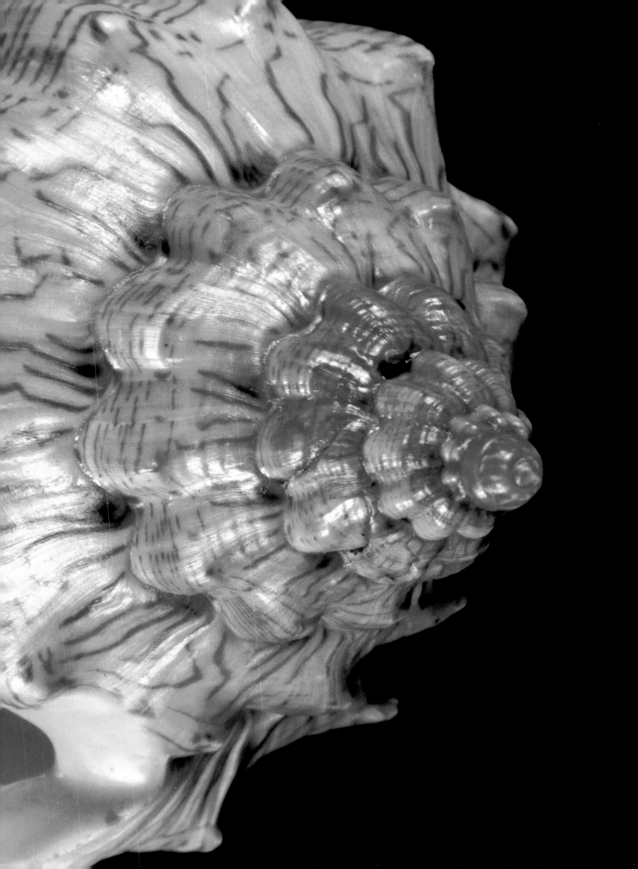

Lyria archeri
(Angas, 1865)

Archer's Lyria

80. *A growth series of the rare* **Lyria archeri** *discovered during the early stages of our searches in 1970. (1.3")*

81 *and* 82. *The charming Music Volute has bars and notes. The shells vary in obesity, the thinner ones being the males. We collected the bright red specimen in Martinique. (3")*

In October of 1969 an exceedingly rare member of the volute family, *Lyria archeri*, was discovered. Known until this time from only a few apparently dead specimens from Montserrat, we found one small colony off the northern end of Guadeloupe. A dozen specimens were collected, most of them inhabited by hermit crabs. These little crustaceans may have killed the *Lyria*, but this cannot be proved; each crab bore bright red eggs, seeming to point towards seasonal spawning. A live *Lyria archeri* was collected at the bottom of marine cliffs in the same area toward nightfall. The mantle was suffused with pink and darker maculations.

The range of this shell would seem confined at present to the islands of the French West Indies and Jamaica.

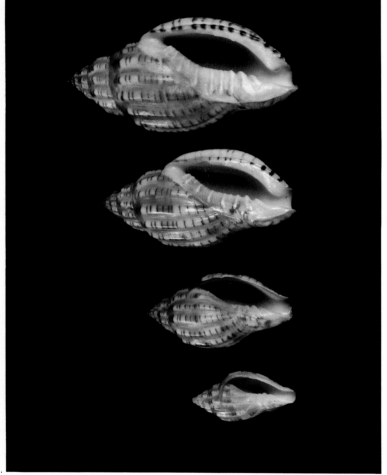

80.

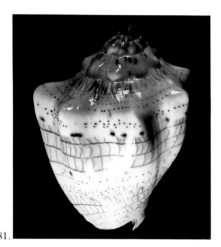

81.

82.

74

Lyria (Enaeta) guildingi
(Sowerby, 1844)
Guilding's Lyria

This is one of the strangest members of the *Volutidae* family. Little is known about the life of this minute member of the subgenus *Enaeta* whose range is from the West Indies to Brazil.

In Martinique came further evidence of their existence. At a depth of 100 feet on sand and coral substrate came two *Lyria guildingi*. There was a live specimen, slightly buried in the sand, and another beside it. On turning over the latter shell it was seen that it had been far less fortunate than its companion. It had been cut in two by some unknown aggressor. Both shells measured five eighths of an inch, body whorls bearing pale maculations on a light brown background; apertures were mauve with one blunt tooth. The orange-yellow coloring mentioned in *Living Volutes* may simply be a variation or loss of color in an older shell. The animal is gray with light speckles.

83. **Lyria (Enaeta) guildingi,** *the smallest member of the family Volutidae in the Caribbean (0.5"). It was named in honor of an English minister, Landsdown Guilding, in 1844.*

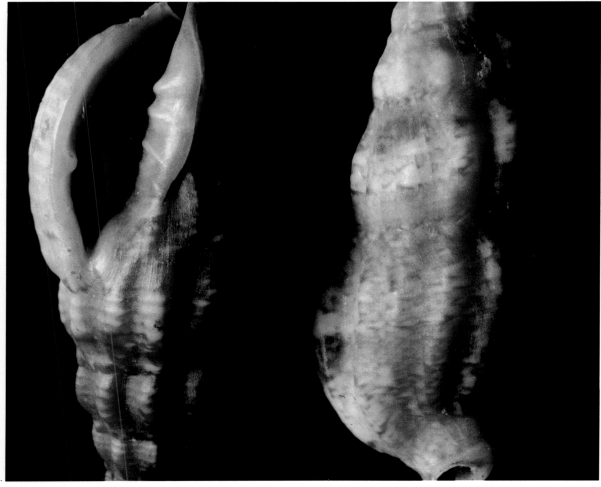

83.

Hindisclava alesidota
(Dall, 1889)

Lean Turrid

The family Turridae has several hundred species in the Caribbean, and their taxonomy is so little known that identification of many species is almost impossible.

Several specimens of this unusual mollusk were collected in the southern part of the range, following dredging operations at Puerto la Cruz, Venezuela, at depths of between 33 and 132 feet. Bottom conditions are reputedly dangerous and visibility down to zero in this area. The eight body whorls are decorated with 17 to 18 longitudinal, strongly beaded ribs which in each case are separated by a deep suture bearing a single axial rib. The outer lip of the aperture is notched at the top showing the characteristic turrid notch of the family.

Conidae

The section to follow is devoted to more than 20 of the more unusual and unexpected qualities of this justifiably much-loved family.

Most of these shells are as at home in the deep waters far from shore as they are in calm, placid bays. Only few are in fact qualified as "deep water dwellers" as most appear to have a surprising ability to live in all conditions and where their fancy takes them. A marked change of color, sculpture, design, finer patterns and shadings have frequently been observed in specimens living at a depth of 100 feet or more.

The West Indian Conidae are greatly affected by environment, and morphological differences within the same species is of so important a nature that constant confusion has arisen in the past when taxonomists and conchologists based their identifications and divisions of species on the outward appearance of the shell, without the evidence of the soft parts. Such has been the case with the variable Caribbean Conidae.

More than 2700 names for the different species have been put forward since Hwass laid down the foundation for the taxonomy of this remarkable genus in 1792, and a count of our Western Atlantic cone shells provides us with more than 180 dubious and obsolete names, synonyms, homonyms, few of which are valid, not to mention misspellings.

This, the most aggressive of gastropods, is capable of injecting an extremely powerful neurotoxin into mollusks, fish and, take heed, humans. I was to witness this on two occasions; it was the brilliantly colored *Conus regius* color form citrinus, which was to show understandable discontent at disruption of its life and habits. The effect of this bite or sting was in many ways comparable to that of the Antillean yellow scorpion — no immediate pain, but a gradual building up of discomfort and a hard swelling which numbs the finger and palm for some hours.

The *Conus spurius* has been reported capable of similar activities. This frightening weapon, with which the cone will paralyze its prey when on predatory travels during nocturnal hours, consists of fine barbs associated with venom. These remain hidden when the cone is at rest, attached to a long coil which nests within the proboscis. The only human deaths from cone stings have occurred in the Indo-Pacific region.

Juvenile cone shells usually resemble the adult; there are exceptions and the young of *Conus ermineus*, *mus* and *regius* have numerous pustules.

84. **Hindsiclava alesidota**
Dall ranges from North Carolina to Barbados in deep water. (0.75")

Caribbean cones are subject to increasing discussion and speculation. Doubt often prevails regarding their identity, owing to the important morphological contrast so apparent in shells from either end of the range. *Conus centurio* well represents this phenomen; the task of separating pale violet or richly orange maculated specimens is a delicate one; serious authors will inform us that in many cases these are the same allied species. *Conus columba* fully illustrates to the reader how one species may vary from island to island.

Conus granulatus
(Linné, 1758)
Glory-of-the-Atlantic Cone

This remarkable cone shell is one of the splendors of the Caribbean molluscan fauna. Little is known of it first discovery. Linné referred to an illustration made by Gualtieri in 1742; Martini ascertained in 1773 that this was an extraordinary shell from the American Indies.

The specimen illustrated is from marine cliffs off Palm Island in the Grenadines and measures two and a quarter inches. Other smaller specimens have been observed at the Saints, Guadeloupe, Martinique and St. Vincent. Brown and white maculated specimens are known to exist in Aruba; pale, almost albino variations, are reported from Bequia. Shells rarely exceed more than two-and-half-inches in length; the range is from Florida and the West Indies. When one spends days beneath the ocean observing and admiring nature's miracles, it is a conchologist's *bête noire* to carry these visions with him or her. To dream by night of confrontations with outstandingly beautiful shells, such as *Conus granulatus*, is one thing, but to come across the object of one's dreams the next morning, hidden under a small triangular rock, is another.

Conus daucus
(Hwass, 1792)
Carrot Cone

This coveted Caribbean cone is one of the most vividly colored of all Conidae. In 1792 Hwass referred to Guadeloupe as the type locality and since that time so many variants have appeared from island to island that many erroneous divisions into species and subspecies have been made.

The Carrot Cone, with its multiple facets, may tend toward lemon and lilac shadings, spots and dashes, white bandings on scarlet and orange body whorls, maculated or unicolored spires; the inner lip may be faded to white, while in a fresh specimen it will be mauve. The animal will be a perfect match when the shell is its usual rich red and sports a minute operculum; the shell bears a distinctive ridged periostracum.

One of the most remarkable and purest in color is a form collected during the study from Diamond Bank, off Martinique. This was the first of many explorations carried out on a bank long ignored owing to strong currents and exposed channel conditions. A Manta Ray whose wing span measured some nine feet, irritated by this unexpected intrusion, gracefully rose from the seabed moving further afield. Before us were the intricate wonders of an undisturbed deep-water reef. Tall barrel sponges harbored dozens of hermit crabs, all active occupants of the empty shells of *Strombus*, Conidae and others.

85. *The scarlet Glory-of-the-Atlantic Cone,* **Conus granulatus,** *is the most sought-after of the Caribbean cones. (3.3")*

Conus daucus
yellow form

This unusual color form of *Conus daucus* comes from the intertidal zone of the Grand Cul-de-Sac of Guadeloupe; the shell shows typical lemon shadings. The delicate lilac form from Corosol, St. Barthelemy, was inhabited by a hermit crab which had carried the shell to the uppermost part of a coral reef. This is what some authors call "*luteus* Krebs", but that name was used earlier by Sowerby for an Indonesian cone.

Conus couderti
(Bernardi, 1860)

This was once considered a rare cone, but in recent years quite a few specimens have been collected by scuba divers in the French Lesser Antilles. It was originally described by the French conchologist Bernardi in 1860 and has since had several names given to it. *Conus archetypus* Crosse, 1863, and *Conus beddomei* Sowerby, 1901, are synonyms.

More than 120 years ago a brilliantly colored specimen was collected in Brazil during Harvard's Thayer Expedition. Dr. William Clench named it *Conus brasiliensis*. Although almost identical to Martinique specimens, some conchologists consider it a subspecies to *couderti*.

The three specimens illustrated here are from coral reefs known as Little Morpion and Punaise in the Grenadine Islands. The cones were buried in fine sand, near small rocks of the intertidal zone; apertures were bright mauve, and all three bore velvety periostracums. The operculums were minute, soft and dark brown.

From the leeward coast of Martinique an astonishing specimen of this species was collected from muddy slopes at a depth of 118 feet by Roget Laurent. Mr Laurent's cone measured two-and-three-quarters inches compared to the shallow water specimens from further south which were one third the size.

Collectors should be wary of confusing hybrid forms of *Conus daucus* with the locally endemic forms of *Conus couderti*.

Conus mindanus
(Hwass in Bruguière, 1792)
Bermuda Cone

This attractive and not too common cone ranges from Bermuda to Florida and throughout the West Indies, usually living on sandy bottoms below low tide line. It has had several synonymic names applied to it, the first being *agassizii* Dall, 1886, the second being *bermudensis* Clench, 1942, and the third being *lymani* Clench, 1942. It also occurs in a fossil form.

The species is quite variable, some being pale and unicolored, while others have delicate series of dots and dashes and red patches on a pale pink background. Measuring one-and-a-quarter inches in length, the two shells illustrated on page 82 were found living together in a small pocket of sand off the village of St. Luce in Martinique. Other specimens were collected in sand at depths of 40 to 100 feet.

86. **Conus daucus** *is probably one of the most variable of the Caribbean cones. (1")*

87. *One of the striking forms of the Carrot Cone is* **luteus.** *One is from Guadeloupe and the other from St. Barthelemy. (1")*

88. *Coudert's Cones also show a great deal of color variation. These came from Little Morpion Island, in the Lesser Antilles. (1")*

86.

87.

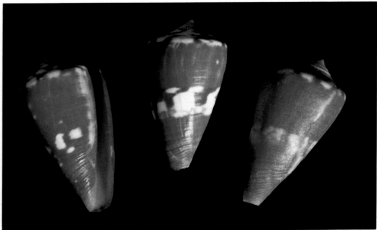

88.

Conus caribbaeus
(Clench, 1942)
Caribbean Cone

Conus caribbaeus is one of the rarest and least understood of West Indian cones. A recent species is described by William J. Clench in *Johnsonia* no. 6, volume 1. The holotype was collected by the late Mr Frank Lyman off Palm Beach, Florida.

Two specimens were collected during the study; one from shallow, inter-tidal waters of the Iles Saintes, at Terre de Haute and the second from 83 feet off the south coast of Martinique. The latter, inhabited by a hermit crab, showed signs of having been the object of considerable aggression during its lifetime, painstakingly repairing the outer lip time and again.

Few records of this cone are known to exist. The 10 to 12 body whorls are somewhat concave on the spire; the main whorl bears eight to ten incised lines near its base as well as fine axial growth lines. The specimen figured here measures one-and-a-quarter inches.

90.

89. *Bermuda Cones in the Caribbean are apt to have delicate speckled patterns. (1.2")*

90. *This badly scarred but rare* **Conus caribbaeus** *is seldom found and looks like a low-spired* **Conus daucus.** *(1")*

Conus columba
(Hwass, 1792)
Dove Cone

Hwass was very affirmative in designating the West Indies as the habitat of this misunderstood and badly documented cone shell. The range is the Greater Antilles and southern Caribbean where it lives on sand and coral bottoms from the intertidal zone to at least 66 feet offshore.

The cone shells featured are delicately colored morphological variants of the snowy white *Conus columba*. The rose-hued form is from deep-water off the leeward coast of Guadeloupe; the pale lavender specimens are from Martinique, a little distance from the littoral of the south coast. The speckled cones come from the western coast of Grenada where specimens favored esturine conditions.

Conus centurio
(Born, 1778)
Centurion Cone

The Centurion Cone illustrated is one of the finest and most valuable examples of the species. It was collected at Diamond Rock from a depth of 132 feet on sand and coral substrates. The body whorl is lilac with irregular bands of brown crossed by deeper-colored flammules.

Other *Conus centurio* collected to the south of this area were morphologically similar to those defined by Usticke as *Conus centurio cruzensis* in his private publication of the listing of cones from St. Croix and the Virgin Islands. Specimens from the Lesser Antilles rarely attain a length of more than one-and-a-quarter inches. The animals of both color forms were similar; the soft parts bright yellow with darker speckling.

91 and 92. The Centurion Cone sometimes has a lilac tinge and chocolate bandings (3"). The one on the right is from Martinique. (3.5")

93. Pastel-colored variants of **Conus columba** *from Caribbean Islands. (1")*

 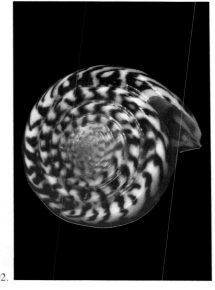

91.   92.

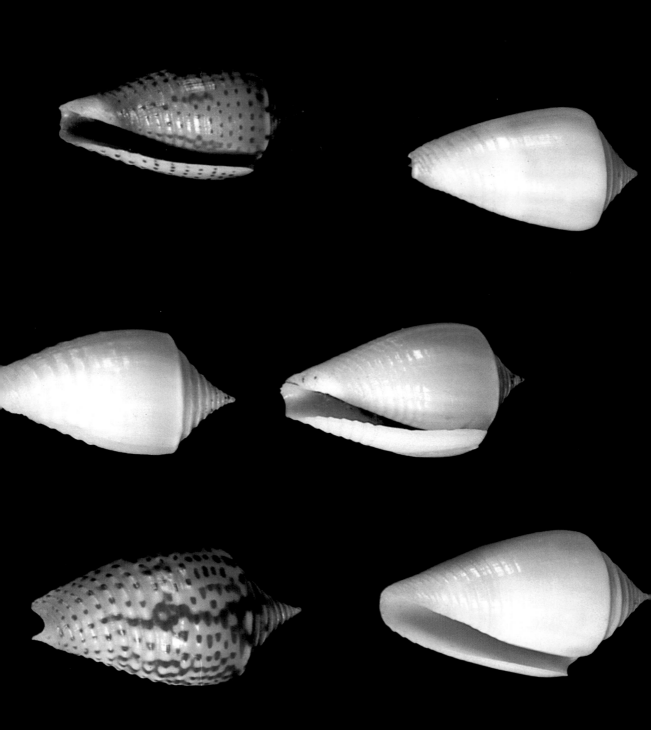

Conus clenchi
(Martins, 1943)
Clench's Cone

The holotype of this very rare and little-known species is found in the Museu Nacional of Brazil, and was collected by E. A. Martins in 1943 at Barra do Fuado, Municipio de Campos, in the State of Rio de Janeiro. In 1970, Rios added Espirito Santo to Puerto Deseado in Argentina as the range of *Conus clenchi*. He records findings made by a fisherman, Leopoldino Pontes, on his two vessels *Pescal 2* and *Santa Maria*. Seven specimens were collected from deep water on sand and mud substrates.

Thought to be an endemic South American cone shell, the solid, brilliant and porcelain-like specimen featured here comes from Martinique. It was recovered from the muddy bottom in the bay of Fort-de-France. This is one of the few color photos of this rarity to be published.

The pattern of the body whorl is distinctive: brown checkering on darker flammules against a pale yellow background; a white mid-band is typical of the species. The few existing specimens of this unusual cone shell measure from one-and-a-quarter to one-and-a-half inches.

Conus regius
(Gmelin, 1791)
Crown Cone

This well-known, striking shell, different from others of Caribbean origin, shows a preference for life among the more turbid waters of our island coastlines. The Crown Cone that chooses a deep, calm dwelling place will attain extraordinary length and perfection of sculpture and design.

The *Conus regius* illustrated here measures three inches and was found on the marine cliff of Horseshoe Reef at Union Island. Morphologically *C. regius* shows considerable variation, induced in many cases by environment. Young specimens resemble the young of *Conus cedonulli* with many pustules on the spiral whorls. The smallest of these juveniles measured an eighth of an inch and was perfectly formed.

Jaimanitas, Cuba, is cited as the type locality in *Johnsonia* although the distribution of this shell ranges from Florida to Brazil.

Conus regius citrinus
(Gmelin, 1791)

Conus regius citrinus is a color form found far less frequently than the ordinary chocolate brown and white-maculated example of this species. It is known to exist throughout the range from Florida Keys to Brazil.

In Martinique, specimens inhabited deep water near offshore reefs. Such cones were entirely yellow with white spires. A little distance away, at 66 feet, the same species of shell existed beneath heavy blocks of coral almost impossible to upturn. The result of having lived in such seclusion was finest sculpturing. Beaded axial ribbing bears numerous prune-colored speckles.

The species possesses an operculum of some importance, taking up from one half to one third of the aperture of the shell. It should be noted that this particular species, *Conus regius citrinus*, has a sting capable of inflicting considerable discomfort for some hours should the barb enter the skin of an unsuspecting collector.

94. *The exceedingly rare* **Conus clenchi** *of the southern Caribbean. (1.7")*

95. *Crown Cones rarely attain the size of this 3-inch giant from an offshore Grenadine reef. The world-record size is 3.4", established in 1985.*

96 and 97. *The yellow form of the Crown Cone,* **Conus regius** *form* **citrinus**, *gave a painful sting to an unsuspecting collector in Martinique. (3")*

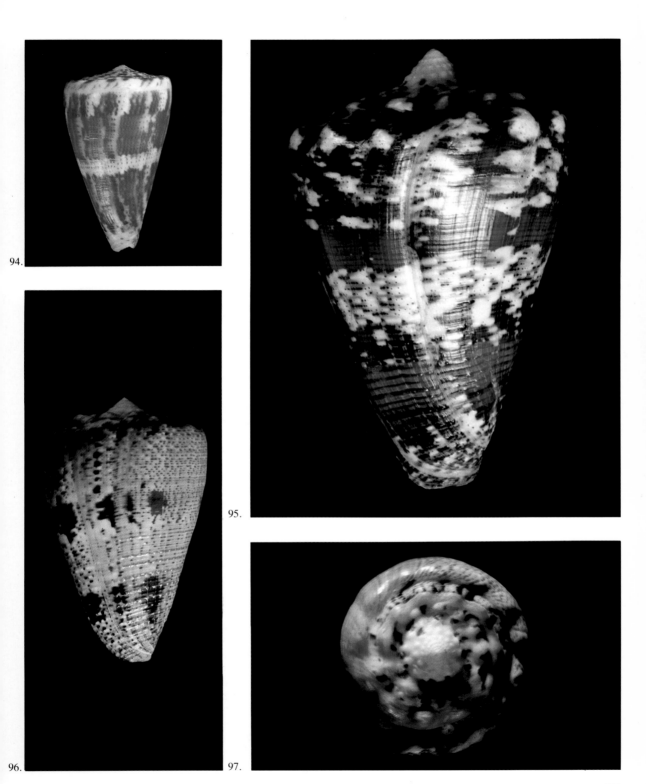

94.

95.

96.

97.

Conus magellanicus
(Hwass in Bruguière, 1792)
The Magellan Cone

This exquisite cone shell rarely exceeds one inch. Its color may vary from pale yellow to fuschia and reddish orange, with irregular white patches centrally and on the spire. Sowerby figures this shell in his *Thesaurus Conchyliorum* of 1858, Part 18, plate 200. At that time he considered it to be a South Australian species, which was an error.

Infrequently encountered in the Lesser Antilles, specimens have been collected in the deeper offshore waters of Martinique in sand and coral substrates at 66 feet, and also from coral reefs in shallow waters of the Tobago Keys in the Grenadines.

Conus ermineus
(Born, 1778)
Turtle Cone

Clench and Bullock reviewed the taxonomy of this unusual West Indian cone in *Johnsonia* in June 1970. They declared *Conus ranunculus* Hwass to be invalid, a name applied to a beach-worn specimen from the Indo-Pacific. The earlier taxon, *Conus ermineus*, was reintroduced to cover an amphi-atlantic species found on both sides of this ocean.

The plump and handsome Turtle Cone may be more or less elusive in the northern part of its range. In Guadeloupe we found little trace of this cone, while small communities were observed off the leeward coasts of all islands south of it. They preferred sand and coral bottoms, often seeking the shelter of small rocky crevices nearby, from depths ranging between 6 and 82 feet. A four-inch specimen tenanted by a hermit crab was found at the base of a marine cliff in the Grenadine islands.

This species has been observed living in pairs. Two specimens were recovered from 165 feet off a lava-clad wreck dating from the eruption of 1902 when the molten flow from Mount Pelee destroyed St. Pierre in Martinique. In these somber environmental conditions the cone shells showed little morphological difference from those of shallow-water origin.

Juveniles are most often pustulate, pink and mauve and fragile in appearance. *Conus verrucosus piraticus* Clench is perhaps none other than the young of *C. ermineus*.

Conus austini
(Rehder and Abbott, 1951)
Austin's Cone

A recently described species, the original *Conus austini* was collected by Waldo L. Schmitt of the *Anton Dohrn* in June of 1932 during dredging operations southeast of Loggerhead Key, Tortugas, Florida, at approximately 40 fathoms. A paratype was dredged at the entrance to English Harbour in Antigua. Since then the range has been extended as far south as Dutch Guiana. This species may be a form of *cancellatus* Hwass.

This graceful cone has a sculpture of some 40 strongly developed spiral cords on the body whorl while the lip is fragile and crenellated. The illustrated specimen was collected at 115 feet from muddy slopes off the Pointe des Negres on the leeward coast of Martinique. This shell is normally all white, but the example given here has slight unusual coloring.

98. *A juvenile (0.75") **Conus magellanicus.**

99 and 101. *The bluish-black coloring of the Turtle Cone is normally covered with a golden periostracum in live specimens. (3.5")*

100. **Conus austini** *is normally whitish but may bear straw-colored stains. It was named after a Smithsonian Institution biologist, Austin Clark. Sometimes called* **cancellatus** *Hwass. (2.8")*

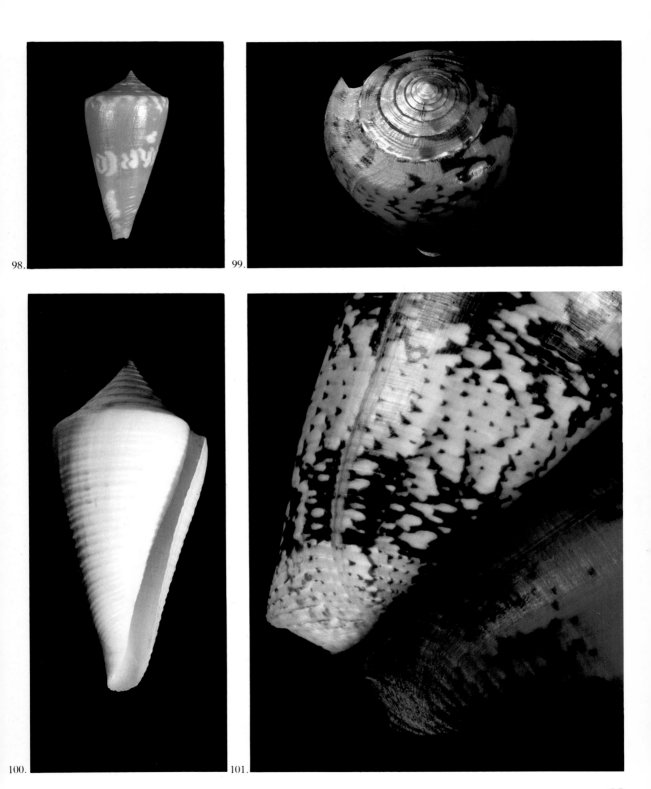

98.

99.

100.

101.

Conus delessertii
(Récluz, 1843)
Sozon's Cone

Conus delessertii, a rare cone in the Caribbean, may be said to have been misunderstood for some time and thought of as a Red Sea species. In 1939 Bartsch created a new taxon, *Conus sozoni*, collected by and named after Mr Sozon Vatikiotis who found the holotype of *C. sozoni* when fishing for sponges on a reef off Tarpon Springs, Florida. *C. sozoni* is now considered a synonym of the original taxon *C. delessertii*.

Over the past 35 years Florida shell collectors, in many cases well equipped and extremely serious in their studies, have provided a considerable amount of material enabling further determination of this and many other species of *Conidae*.

Conus delessertii is very common off the east coast of Florida: three distinct bands of zigzag orange markings on white, a high spire and elongate form distinguish this shell which in many ways resembles the *Conus centurio* found in Martinique. Adults attain a length of four inches.

Conus attenuatus
(Reeve, 1844)
Usticke's Cone

Morphologically this uncommon and colorful cone varies considerably within populations. When first encountered it was difficult not to divide the species. Younger specimens were glossy white with pale yellow flammules and high-spired, while adults were orange or deep pink. Usually these colorations formed thick spiral bands on a paler background, the body whorl bearing strong sculpturing near its base. The periostracum is thick, hiding the general color and pattern of the shell. A minute operculum is present and the much-flattened spire bears red flammules. The periostracum is fine with hairlike protrusions on the keel of the last whorl.

This sand-loving cone is found more usually on marine cliffs and has, in most cases, been collected living in pairs in 65 to 100 feet on sand. Those figured here come from Carriacou, Grenada, while others have been observed living on the offshore reefs.

This inch-long cone was originally named after Gordon Usticke who did much to further our knowledge of the Virgin Island fauna.

Conus cedonulli
(Linné 1758)
subsp. caracanus
(Hwass in Bruguière 1792)

One of the handsomest of all Antillean Conidae is *Conus cedonulli* subspecies *caracanus*, considered in its early days as an Indo-Pacific species. Mörch was to elucidate matters in 1852 when he described a synonymous member of the genus from the Netherland Antilles. It is a rare subspecies frequently confused with the true *Conus cedonulli*; an understandable error as both cone shells are endemic to the southern Caribbean.

In early life the young *C. caracanus* will appear slender and high-spired; many such specimens are bright mauve. Both juveniles and adults possess as many as 90 to 100 dots per inch on the raised spiral lines decorating the

102. **Conus delessertii** *is quite rare in the West Indies, but off east Florida it is commonly dredged by commercial scallop fishermen. It may be a northern subspecies of* **Conus centurio***. (2.5")*

10

glossy body whorl; these will be alternately brown or black and white, or the background color of the body whorl and white. There is no outlining of the painted patches as with the *C. cedonulli*. The animal is scarlet with microscopic white flecks; the operculum minute and almost invisible in the smaller shells.

The largest of these specimens measured three-and-one-eighths inches. Most adult shells attain a length of two-and-three-eighths inches. The subspecies or form occurs in the Grenadines and Netherland Antilles.

Conus cedonulli
(Linné, 1767)
The Matchless Cone

Ranking among the most coveted of rare cone shells, the extravagant and novel *Conus cedonulli* (from the Latin "I yield to none") of 18th-century fame, was for many years the gem of the collections of the Kings of France and Portugal.

Lovell Reeve in Volume 1 of his *Conchologia Iconica* describes in great detail the different aspects of this stunning shell: ". . . turbinated, either orange or olive yellow, olive chestnut or purple black . . . irregularly painted with white spots, disjointed or flowing together . . ." He continues "such are the normal characters of this far-famed cone, but so variably are they developed in every specimen that I have examined that to be able to establish a strict conventional set of varieties is beyond all hope". Reeve gives an extremely detailed account of seven varieties.

Deep-water dwellers in general and rarely cast ashore, the shell is highly prized by collectors; its rarity and unsurpassed beauty have been extolled by writers from Klein to the present day; the same feeling of wonder comes over the neophyte or student who may handle this handsome cone shell for the first time.

The locality of *Conus cedonulli* for this particular study is St. Vincent. Dredging operations in Kingstown Harbour yielded a number of specimens from the muddy substrate at a depth of 66 to 132 feet, typical of a port. Juvenile and adult shells were collected from eel-grass beds off Palm Island in the Grenadines and sandy substrates at Port Halifax, Grenada.

The even rarer dark chestnut specimens figured here are known as the forma *holemani*, after John Holeman of New York, whose methodical research and love of cones is unequalled. An adult *Conus cedonulli* may attain two-and-three-eighths inches.

Terebra taurinus
(Lightfoot, 1786)
Flame Auger

This is the most beautiful of the Atlantic *Terebra*. Its long slender shell appears to be clothed with many tongues of fire along its entire length. The tiny cream-colored mollusk displays great strength as it ambles houseborn over sand and muddy substrates in deep shadowy waters.

Living in small groups, this much-coveted *Terebra* is nocturnal, trapping other small mollusks and unsuspecting invertebrates with its efficient stinging apparatus. Few members of this elegant species exist in the Caribbean. Ranging from Florida to the West Indies and Brazil, adult shells may reach a length of at least six inches.

103. **Conus attenuatus** *in the young form has an elevated spire, but in the adults (1.5") the spires are low.*

104. *The variety* **caracanus** *is a dark form of* **Conus cedonulli,** *the Matchless Cone. (2")*

105. *(opposite page). Some of Reeve's 1849 descriptions of the Matchless Cone in his work,* **Conchologia Iconica,** *apply to the handsome modern-day specimens. (3")*

Polystira albida
(Perry, 1811)
Giant White Turrid

Few shells have the graceful lines of the exquisite *Polystira albida*. Purest white spiral cords decorate the body whorls and the aperture bears a distinctive deep notch and a sickle-shaped operculum.

We have observed this shell in company with *Terebra taurinus* and *Strombus pugilis* living in moderately deep water. A member of the very advanced group of *Turridae*, and capable of adapting themselves to all conditions in both temperate and tropical seas, the Giant White Turrid has been observed living in deep bays off Martinique, St. Lucia and St. Vincent. The range of this species extends from Florida down to Brazil where Rios has made note of its presence.

Crassipira species

This large *Crassipira* species comes from the same habitat of muddy substrate as the *Polystira* and *Terebra shells*. It was tenanted by a hermit crab which put its head down in order to make itself look as insignificant as possible at our approach. Unfortunately for the crab, the shell it bore was too unusual a specimen for us to resist collecting.

Most members of genus *Crassispira* are some five-eighths of an inch in length and occasionally will grow beyond one-and-a-quarter inches. In this case the gastropod had attained a length of one-and-five-eighths inches with 14 oblique sharply bladed ribs per whorl crossed by wavy lines. The deep suture between the eight body whorls was heavily frilled and measured one third of the length of each of these. The columella was smooth and glossy, the outer lip thickened. This Turridae was collected in the bay of Fort de France in November 1972.

106 and 107. The beauty of the spotting of the Flame Auger is usually hidden by a brownish periostracum. (3.5" and 4")

108. Incomparable elegance and purity of swirling lines mark this exquisite all-white Giant White Turrid. (2")

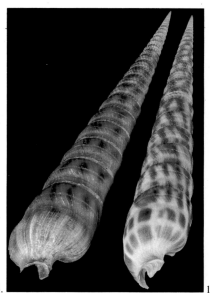

106.

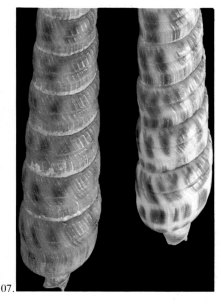

107.

Micromelo undata
(Bruguière, 1792)

Miniature Melo

Algae serve as the base of the marine food chain and are the grazing ground of one of the most exquisite of the smaller West Indian mollusks, the Miniature Melo. This seldom-seen, beautiful invertebrate was found in Martinique. The delicate shell has a mantle of palest yellow, speckled with mauve and edged with phosphorescent blue.

This little fellow was active and very friendly. During its time in the laboratory aquarium it dozed during the night, making hay during the daylight hours. We became very attached to him and were to grieve his imprudence one day when he disappeared down the aeration pipe.

The shell is fragile and almost transparent, with dark red lines and threads on a lilac-colored background. Our largest specimen, collected in 1971, measured half an inch and came from the sand and coral bottom at 50 feet off the west coast of Martinique.

109. This **Crassispira** *turrid led a precarious life as the scars on the body show. (1.5")*

110. and 111. The tiny bubble shell, **Micromelo undata,** *lives among green algae and is one of the most fragile of all West Indian mollusks. (0.5")*

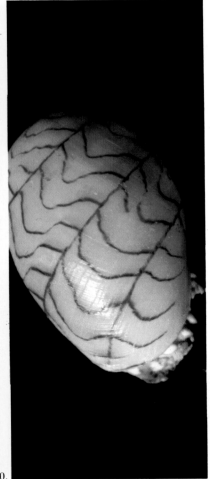

110.

111.

99

113.

Bivalvia

Chlamys imbricata
(Gmelin, 1791)
Little Knobby Scallop

One of the most elegant of all bivalve shells, the Little Knobby Scallop has prune-colored flutings on the numerous ribs which are matched by as many as 26 shining brown eyes with many red lashes and several speckled, retractable tentacles.

One to two inches in length when adult, this *Chlamys* shows preference for life in caves and grottos where the most perfect specimens enjoy a peaceful existence at 66 to 100 feet. Shallow-water dwellers will rarely display the same perfection of color and sculpturing.

Usually attached in much the same way as its neighbor, the handsome *Lima 'lima*, the scallop when disturbed will make off in the opposite direction, quickly detaching itself and clapping its valves in order to swim to a safer, deeper niche. This choice scallop is moderately common from Bermuda and southeastern Florida to the lower Caribbean.

Lyropecten nodosus
(Linné, 1758)
Lion's Paw

Lyropecten nodosus is among the largest and most colorful of all the West Indian scallops. It has a near relative in the Gulf of California and the Galapagos.

The Lion's Paw has endeavored to keep its habitat a secret; communities were encountered in one channel area at 100 feet. Seas were northeasterly, currents strong and shelter poor. Many scarlet and orange valves from these populations are eventually cast shoreward, to be found on beaches off the northern tip of Guadeloupe. In Martinique and St. Vincent this bivalve was present in semi-enclosed bays where wave action was negligible and the shells smaller.

Chlamys multisquamata
(Dunker, 1864)
Many-Ribbed Scallop

Rarest and most vivid of the North and South American scallops, this unusual and beautiful bivalve originates from deep-water dredgings off Havana, Cuba. It favors the obscurity of waters some distance from the littoral and is endemic to many of the Lesser Antillean islands. Fine laminations decorate the numerous ribs of both valves; magnificent in their flashing rainbow shades of pinks and mauves, startling yellows and orange, the inner valves are faintly iridescent.

Crevices of marine cliffs some 100 feet beneath the ocean's surface are this rare creature's stronghold. Several specimens were found covered with sediment and a fine mossy-green periostracum; empty shells could be seen in the early morning after the night passage of other cliff tenants.

112. *These fan-shaped* **Chlamys imbricata** *are rock-dwelling scallops renowned for their intricate scaling. (1.2")*

113. *The colorful Lion's Paw,* **Lyropecten nodosa,** *ranges from S.E. United States to Brazil and Ascension Island. Rarely it may be lemon yellow. (3.5")*

114. *Lost to collectors for over a century,* **Chlamys multisquamata** *was known from only one Cuban specimen from 1864 until rediscovered in 1970. (2.5")*

Tellina radiata
(Linné, 1758)

color form *unimaculata*
(Lamarck, 1818)

White Sunrise Tellin

The snowy-colored *Tellina radiata unimaculata* was named by Lamarck in volume V of his *Animaux sans Vertebres*. He considered that the purity of the shell's albinism made it very distinct from the magnificent sunrise shadings of the other members of *Tellina radiata* Linné.

The type specimen is from Montego Bay, Jamaica; here the *T. unimaculata* is not as rare as in the southern Caribbean. Only one or two specimens have been recovered from the offshore waters of these islands of the Lesser Antilles.

Tellins are an ancient variety of shells; the name *tellen* is known to have been used in the first century by Dioscorides of Anazarba.

115. *The largest Caribbean tellin,* **Tellina magna.** *(8")*   115.

Tellina magna
(Spengler, 1798)
Great Tellin

This handsome *Tellin* is considered rare in many areas of the Caribbean. It may be detected by two small holes which indicate the presence of the slender siphons with which the clam filters fresh seawater.

This bivalve was first encountered off the coasts of Guadeloupe and Dominica and favoured fine coral sands 60 feet beneath the ocean's surface. Specimens collected were in some cases uniformly peach-colored but the left valve is usually glossy white. The species occurs from Bermuda and southern Florida to the West Indies.

Spondylus ictericus
(Reeve, 1856)
Digitate Thorny Oyster

Not to be confused with the long-spined *Spondylus americanus* which is a close relative, *Spondylus ictericus* has chunky short spines that are digitate, even in the smallest of specimens. Less abundant, the Digitate Thorny Oyster lives in shallow water often among eel-grass, on pilings near piers and sometimes attached to small rocks.

The handsome shell illustrated here lived by itself in a nest of seaweed in the calm waters of the Grand Cul-de-Sac of Guadeloupe, with a mossy-green periostracum by way of camouflage. Searching on many subsequent occasions in this same area did not indicate the presence of others.

Usually measuring two inches, the shells may vary from pinkish white, prune and mauve with paler digitations, to orange and vermilion. Often the shell is scarlet with bright yellow thorns.

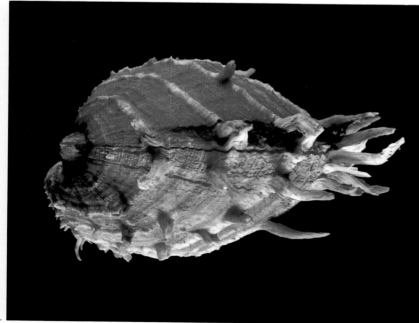

116.

116. *Usually found sparsely inhabiting the offshore reef cliffs, the Digitate Thorny Oyster is amply protected by a strong, brightly-colored shelly box. (2.3")*

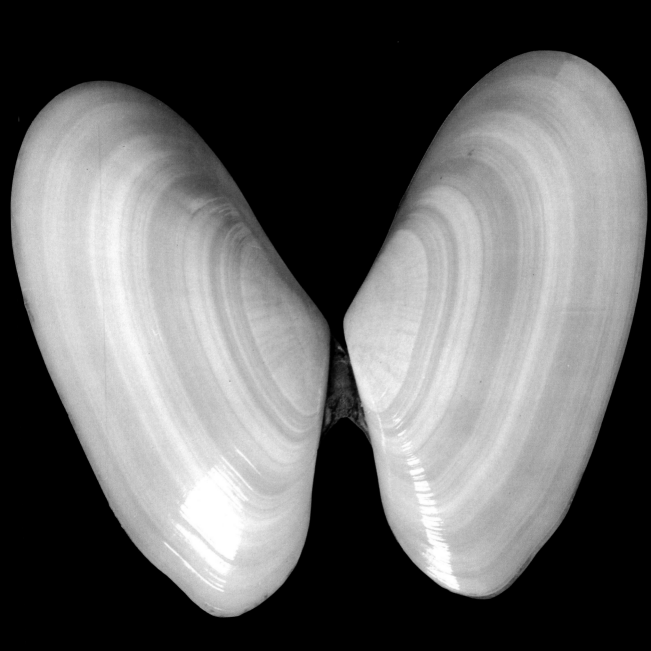

118.

Spondylus americanus
(Hermann, 1781)
Atlantic Thorny Oyster

Found in deep and murky waters of marine cul-de-sacs, the delicate long-spined thorny oyster is unrecognizable in its natural surroundings. Covered with *Parazoa* sponges and an amazing number of small marine fellow creatures, it escapes even the practised eye. The quick snapping shut of the two valves, as the mollusk senses imminent danger with the change of light, will give its presence away.

The animal is blood red, its mantle fringed with white and brown maculations. Colonies are gradually diminishing in size because of intensive over-collecting owing to the extraordinary beauty of the pastel-hued shell.

They are filter feeders and easy prey to *Murex*. The oyster will try to shake the predator off, opening and shutting its valves at a speed that is difficult to imagine unless witnessed.

Pitar dione
(Linné, 1758)
Royal Comb Venus

In the southern Caribbean and Lesser Antilles in general this exquisite bivalve is a rarity, while it appears to be moderately common in the Greater Antilles. From the Venezuelan coastal islands specimens were collected near shore from muddy bottoms.

The delicate long spines which characterize the valves are absent in all other West Indian bivalves. The glassy, concentric ridges may be either pink, white or mauve. Adult shells may attain two inches in length.

Chione cancellata
(Linné, 1758)
form *mazycki* Dall, 1902

117. *Resembling a butterfly, the white color form of the Sunrise Tellin lacks the rosy rays of its brothers and sisters. (2.8")*

118. *As the very old American Spiny Oyster grew, it retained a thick, curled early section to its shell. (6")*

119. *Extravagant crowns of upturned frills bedeck the valves of colorful variants of* **Chione cancellata,** *a common venus clam. (1")*

120. *This rare and delicate deepwater* **Chazalie's** *Scallop is 1 inch in size. Its valve on the right is cup-shaped while the left or upper one is flat.*

121. *A diffused pearly sheen enhances the bright inside of the valve of this mysterious Gari clam. (1.4")*

Three bivalves not generally known to collectors of West Indian mollusks were gathered in 1973. Two of these were from 100 feet on sand and coral substrates off the south coast of Martinique and sported pairs of wings on the final concentric lamellae.

The shell has between 30 and 32 gently rounded ribs and ten frilled and upturned concentric lamellae with deep pink stripes on a paler background. The rosy, heart-shaped lunule is crossed by red threads and the escutcheon is almond-shaped with numerous brown zigzag markings. It is a deep-water color form of the common Ribbed Venus.

Genus *Gari*
(Schumacher, 1817)
Subgenus *Gobraeus*
(Brown, 1844)

This brilliant rose-colored bivalve shell, with translucent pearly inner valves splashed with white, is a member of a little known genus unaccounted for in West Indian waters. Several species of the genus *Gari* are known from the western coast of America and Eastern Pacific regions.

Two specimens of the subgenus *Gobraeus* were collected on sand and coral substrates in 60 feet of water from the leeward coasts of Mayero Island

and Martinique. Specimens measured one-and-a-half and two inches. Outer valves were adorned with numerous concentric threads which tended to dull the outward appearance of the shell. When closed the valves are seen to have a typical open gape at the posterior end.

The Eastern Pacific species, *G. helenae*, resembles it very closely. This may be *Gari vaginoides* (Reeve)

Pecten chazaliei
(Dautzenberg, 1900)
Chazalie Scallop

The Chazalie Scallop is a fairly recent taxon resulting from Dautzenberg's studies in 1900 which has been dredged on infrequent occasions in a few areas of the Antillean range.

Three exquisite specimens were collected during this study in 60 feet of water in fine sand and coral substrate off the southern coast of Grenada. The rich zigzag markings of the right, or upper (shown on the left in our picture) valve of the species illustrated is an added perfection in what is normally a pale, unicolored shell. The lower or left valve is inflated, translucent and decorated with many ribs flecked with fawn on a series of finest wine-colored longitudinal threads. The scallops measured five-eighths to one inch.

122. *The Royal Comb Venus; their spines assist them in remaining safely buried in shallow-water sands. (1.5")*

119. 120. 121.

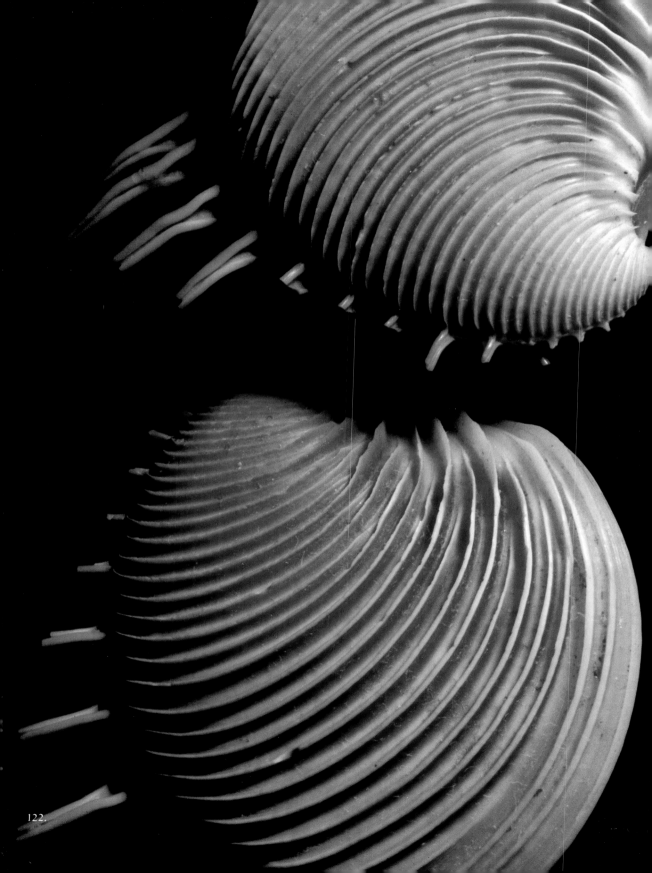

4

Science in shells

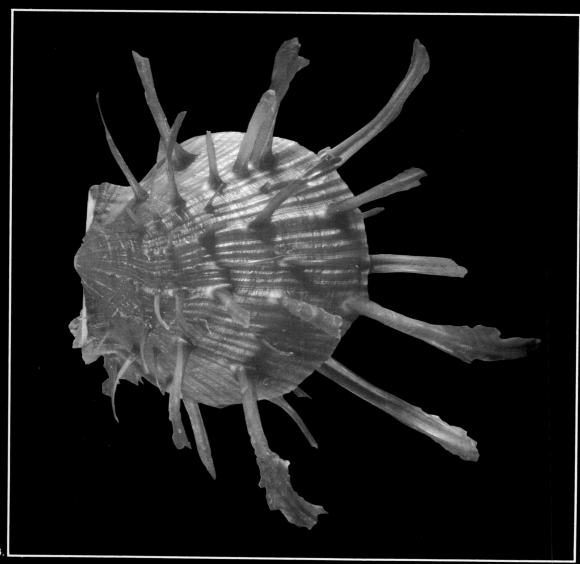

Science in shells
Oceanographic voyages for shells

Toward the close of the 18th century a very real interest developed for the molluscan fauna of the Antillean province. France was leader and her patron the Paris Museum of Natural History.

The fortunate scientists who were to contemplate many new wonders from the ocean for the first time sailed aboard three- and four-masted brigantines on which living conditions were often harsh, the elements frequently wearing and tropical ills fatal to weakened bodies. Many of the early oceanographers reached little more than middle age, often leaving behind them monumental texts as proof of their passionate devotion to the study of ocean life.

Between 1830 and 1840 the French vessels *Venus* and *Astrolabe* circumnavigated the globe by way of the West Indies, collecting many hundreds of mollusks that were new to science. In 1831, H.M.S. *Beagle* set sail from Plymouth with no less a person aboard than the young and brilliant Charles Darwin; he was prone to that most dismal malady, seasickness, but nonetheless remained faithful to his five-year assignment. The Beagle was to first touch land at San Salvador, Bahia; few forms of nature escaped the quick eye of Darwin, and beautiful illustrations — including those of mollusks — were to accompany the long texts that were the outcome of so complete a voyage.

Perhaps the most outstanding oceanographic expedition supported by the Royal Society and Gladstone's government, was that of the corvette *Challenger*. In 1872, when the *Challenger* set to sea, her commission was the pursuit of the most priceless of all acquisitions — knowledge, featuring oceanography as a science in its own right. She was a three-masted square rigger of some 2,300 tons and 200 feet overall; a steamship with an engine of more than 1,200 h.p. Two of the 17 original guns remained to protect her. All told she sailed 68,000 nautical miles — the equivalent of nearly three times the circumference of the globe.

Wyville Thompson was the senior natural historian aboard; patiently he organized and witnessed the soundings and dredging of the ocean depths while crossing the Atlantic. All hands were occupied to sound and maneuver machines each 200 miles; 45 minutes was required for the sounding of 3,000 fathoms; it took three hours of manual work on windlasses to dredge the abyssal depths some 2,500 fathoms below. Amidst considerable rejoicing on the part of the crew, the *Challenger* berthed at St. Thomas in the Virgin Islands on March 16, 1873 after an arduous crossing.

It was from St. Thomas, in fact, that the richest hauls were made throughout the entire voyage. The outcome of this epic journey was 50 large volumes explaining the ocean's resources as seen by the scientific team aboard. Volumes I and II, published in 1877, are devoted to the Atlantic and Caribbean islands. Another outcome was that more than 90 members of the crew abandoned ship before she returned to Spithead in 1876; they chose the joyful life and pleasurable living with island maidens.

The West Indian seas were of particular interest to the new American colonies. Support for research in the Gulf of Mexico, Atlantic and Caribbean was forthcoming. A year later the U.S. Survey steamer *Blake*

123. *American Spiny Oyster,* **Spondylus americanus.** *(5.5")*

112

was to devote her navigational and research activities entirely to the Caribbean and Gulf of Mexico until 1880. Alexander Agassiz supervised the operations, and William Healey Dall, a leading authority on the molluscan fauna, devoted many years to a better knowledge of what had been a much neglected province up until that time. Few "stones" were left unturned and went as far as deep-sea dredging the bathymetric zone.

Dall was greatly aided by the Challenger reports, edited by the Reverend Boog Watson; of much value were the works of Dr Paul Fischer resulting from the journeys of the French vessels *Talisman* and *Travailleur*. "The magnitude of our knowledge of the mollusks of the region" says Dall, "is due to the exertions of Professors Agassiz, Pourtales, Sigsbee, Bartlett and their co-workers."

More than 1,000 species were recovered by the *Blake*, one half of them for the first time. It was observed that the relation of the deep sea fauna was closest to that of the Tertiary rather than to the fauna of the littoral. Dall found difficulty in setting the limits of the divisions and boundaries of the fauna. In all cases the richest areas were the archibenthal regions skirting the continental shores or islands. The deep-sea species were beautiful and delicate, often pustulate and transparent, qualities not present in shallow-water specimens. Dall considered many mollusks existed at depths too great to allow algae of any sort to flourish.

What may be observed today is that there is an important richness on marine cliffs which descend sharply from 50 to 330 feet — as in the case of Diamond Rock and Kick'm Jenny. Both display an extraordinary variety of fauna over their entire face before reaching the seabed, or the main plateau of impalpable mud. Areas off the volcanic shores of islands bear a strange resemblance to what could be considered abyssal conditions. From 66 feet only rare or unusual forms of *echinids* are present. Albino turrids and *Fusinus* shells and fragile bivalve specimens are almost impossible to collect. The molluscan fauna varied enormously to that found at similar depths in association with coralline substrates.

Dall concluded pleasantly that Pliocene and Miocene shells of Tertiary origin were, in all evidence, still happily alive and thriving on the abyssal sea bed. Modern studies suggest that the difference between shallow water and abyssal species is not as great as Dall claimed.

124. *One of the world's most beautiful mariner's graveyards is located at Terre de Haut, Iles des Saintes. Each grave is bordered with pink* **Strombus gigas** *and masses of rose-colored "soucie" flowers.*

The scientific study of the Caribbean molluscan fauna

The most important amassment of scientific material referring directly to the Western Atlantic molluscan fauna was that gathered by William Stimpson (1832—1872) during his time as Director of the Chicago Academy of Sciences.

Stimpson was a well-travelled scientist and had obtained the generous help of more public and private collections, museums and foundations than had any of his co-workers before him; the quality and quantity of marine species from the eastern United States and Caribbean was the most remarkable collection gathered together under one roof. It represented thousands of hours of research by individuals throughout little-known areas of the ocean depths. The manuscript undertaken by Stimpson, and nearing completion by 1871, was a work of more than monumental order, containing hundreds of fine engravings and illustrations and descriptions of numerous new species. It certainly was to be one of the richest malacological works of the century.

Within sight of the end of his strenuous labors, a shattering catastrophe was to strike Chicago and with it Stimpson's Academy of Sciences. The great fire of October 8, 1871 swept through the city, consuming the entire collection of specimens and Stimpson's years of devoted labor. The shock was so great for Stimpson that he died in a state of grave depression some few months later on May 26, 1872 at the age of 40.

Charles B. Adams (1814—1853), Professor of Zoology at Amherst College, Massachusetts, for years devoted himself to studying the many small and fascinating mollusks of the sublittoral zones of Panama, Jamaica and the Virgin Islands. His numerous field trips resulted in monographs and reviews of many species. An incorrigible zoologist, he continued his study of these small animals while suffering from yellow fever on the island of St. Thomas and died while working at the age of 39 on January 18, 1853. He was buried at St. Thomas.

The lot of malacologists is, however, not constantly fraught with such unhappy stories. Some 10 years after the death of Stimpson, Dall was able to pick up the task left unfinished with more good fortune than his predecessor. Charles Johnson (1863—1932) was prolific in his writings and contributions on the molluscan fauna of the Atlantic coast.

Dr. William J. Clench (1897—1984) indulged in the pleasures of unravelling the many mysteries of Caribbean gastropods and bivalves. He was editor and founder of the most valuable of all modern works on Western Atlantic mollusks, *Johnsonia* and *Occasional Papers on Mollusks* printed by Harvard University. These papers systematically reviewed new and obsolete species, synonyms, types, ranges and habitats. They put better order into the often confusing records of cones, murexes, and other misunderstood members of the phylum.

William Clench may be thought of as one of the most outstanding personalities of the century with regard to his important scientific contributions to the study of molluscan fauna of the Americas, leaving his mark on malacological history in a way that Linné, Lamarck and Dall had done before him.

125. *Even 20 million years ago shells were experimenting with new approaches. Here is the left-handed coiling, or sinistral, species.* **Conus adversarius** *from southern Florida. (1.5")*

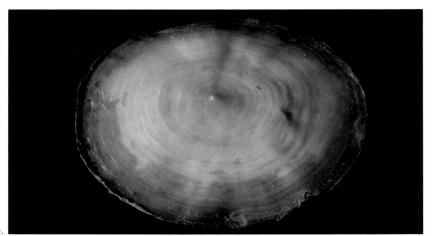

126.

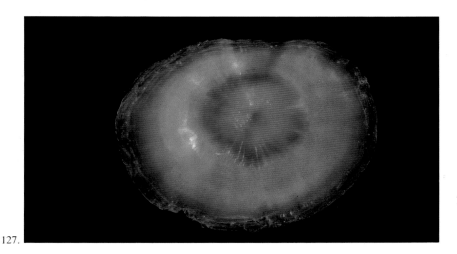

127.

126 and 127. *Although resembling knee-cap bones, these shells belong to the opisthobranch snail,* **Umbraculum umbraculum.** *Early naturalists were perplexed about their origin. (2.8")*

128. **Cypraea problematica** *from the Pliocene beds of Florida retain their colorful luster despite their 20 million years of age. (2")*

129. *One of the rarest of all shell objects in the history of Antillean archaeology is this carving representing both male and female Arawak deities (8") probably from a* **Strombus costatus** *shell.*

128.

131.

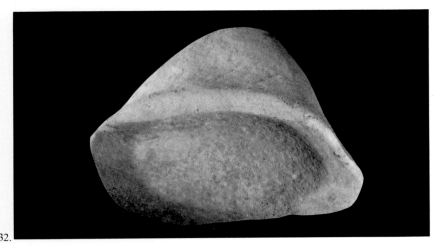

132.

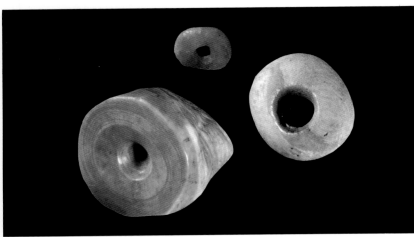

133.

130. *An Arawak goddess in pendant form was once worn by a young Indian mother more than a thousand years ago. Atabeyra, or the Frog Lady, represents fertility and is seen in a birth-giving position.*

131. *A Glycymeris clam, possibly* **G. americanus** *from Florida, was found in archaeological excavations in the Grenadines. (1.5")*

132. *Amerindians protected themselves from the evil spirits by "Zemis" or "three-cornered stones" fashioned from the shell spines of conch shells. These cult objects may be compared to the Christian crucifix. (1.5")*

133. *Recently discovered archet tools from Indian burial sites were used for making beads and piercing them with holes.*

134. *Wentletraps were greatly sought after by early connoisseurs of conchology. These* **Epitonium albidum** *are sand dwellers. (1.5")*

119

Bibliography, Index and Glossary of shell terms

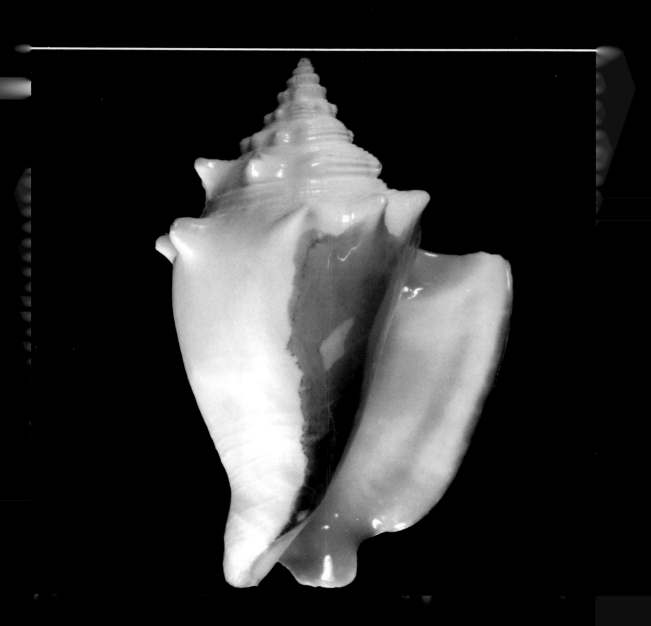

Bibliography

Abbott, R. Tucker. 1958. The Marine Mollusks of Grand Cayman Island, West Indies. Monograph 11, Academy of Natural Sciences of Philadelphia.

Abbott, R. Tucker. 1974. American Seashells, 2nd edition. Van Nostrand/Reinhold, NY.

Abbott, R. Tucker. 1984. Collectible Shells of Southeastern U.S. Bahamas and Caribbean. American Malacologists, Inc., Melbourne, Florida.

Abbott, R. Tucker and S. Peter Dance. 1982. Compendium of Seashells. E. P. Dutton, NY.

Bullock, Robert C. 1974. A contribution to the systematics of some West Indian *Latirus* (Gastropoda: Fasciolariidae). The Nautilus, vol. 88, no. 3, pp. 69–89.

Carriker, Melbourne R. 1972. Observations on the removal of spines by muricid gastropods during shell growth. The Veliger, vol. 15, no. 2, pp. 69–74.

Clarke, Arthur H. 1962. Annotated List and Bibliography of the Abyssal Marine Mollusks of the World. National Museum of Canada, Bull. 181.

Clench, William J. (editor). 1941–80. Johnsonia. Monographs of Marine Mollusca of the Western Atlantic. Vol. 1–4. Harvard, Mass.

Clench, William J. and R. D. Turner. 1941–81. Occasional Papers on Mollusks. Vols. 1–4. Harvard Univ., Cambridge, Massachusetts.

Dall, William, H. 1886 and 1889. Reports on the Results of Dredging — Steamer 'Blake'. Bull. Museum Comp. Zoology, Harvard, vol. 12, 18.

Dugast, Abbé. 1767. *Raisons et systématiques des curiosités de la nature et de l'art trouvé dans le cabinet M. Davila*. Paris.

Dance, S. Peter. 1966. Shell Collecting — an Illustrated History. Faber and Faber, London.

Humfrey, Michael. 1975. Sea Shells of the West Indies. Collins, London.

Lamarck, J.B.P. A. de Monet. 1801. *Système des Animaux sans Vertèbres*. Paris.

Long, Glenn A. 1974. Frog motifs on archaeological mollusks of Hokokam and Mogollan cultures. The Nautilus, vol. 88, pp. 47–51.

135. *The Fighting Conch,* **Strombus pugilis**, *is normally a beautiful orange color, but one in ten thousand may have a pure white shell. The animal is usually colored in all cases. (3.4")*

136. *Details showing the siphonal canals of two* **Fusinus marmoratus** *(Philippi) from Venezuela. (4")*

137. *A* **Spondylus americanus** *is aged and comfortably installed in the arms of an old coral frond. (5")*

136.

Marsh, J. A. and O. M. Rippingale. 1974. Cone shells of the World. 3rd. ed. Jacaranda Press, Sydney.

Percharde, Peter L. 1972. Observations on the gastropod, *Charonia variegata*, in Trinidad and Tobago. The Nautilus, vol. 85, pp. 84–90.

Pitman, R. W. 1976. Journey to Falcon — the story of *Cypraea mus*.

Reeve, Lovell A. and G. B. Sowerby (2nd). 1843–78 *Conchologia Iconica*. 20 vols. London.

Rios, Eli C. 1975. Brazilian Marine Mollusks Iconography. Museu Oceanograf. do Rio Grande, Brazil.

Rumphius, G. E. 1705. *D'Amboinsche Rariteitkamer.* Amsterdam, 2nd edition, 1741.

Sowerby, G. B. (1st, 2nd & 3rd), 1842–87. *Thesaurus Conchyliorum*, or monographs of genera of shells. 5 vol. London.

Shuster, Carl N., Jr. and W. T. Bode. 1962. Observations on *Vasum globulus nuttingi* with comments on other Caribbean Vase Shells. The Nautilus. vol. 75, pp. 1–7.

Thompson, Sir Wyville C. 1877. Voyage of the Challenger: the Atlantic. Vols. 1 and 2, London.

Waller, Thomas. 1971. The habits and habitats of some Bermudian marine mollusks. The Nautilus, vol. 87, no. 2, pp. 31–52.

Warmke, Germaine and R. T. Abbott. 1961. Caribbean Seashells. Dover Publications, NY.

Warmke, Germaine. 1960. Seven Puerto Rico cones: notes and radulae. The Nautilus, vol. 73., pp. 119–124.

Weaver, Clifford S, and J. du Pont. 1970. The Living Volutes. Delaware Museum of Natural History, Greenville, Delaware.

138. *Man's desire for protein food in remote islands is putting pressure on the populations of the Pink Conch,* **Strombus gigas.**

138.

Acknowledgements

My most heartfelt thanks are extended to the late Raymond Gaillot; without his sound advice and without the generous aid of his staff and photographic laboratory this book could never have been possible. To Philippe Margolis, a patient bystander and contributor, whose boats and expertise over a period of nine years were always at hand to help navigate and explore; to Bernard Salvat my eternal thanks for unfailing encouragement in this endeavor; to Dr. Thomas Waller of the Smithsonian Institution my sincere recognition for his valuable time in the identification of the bivalve specimens; to Dave and Kani Meyers and Dr. Brad Macurda my thanks for the introduction to many new forms of marine life; to Dr. Tom Thompson for patient correspondence from afar to elucidate the habits of certain opistobranchia; to Janine Dhuicq and Roget Laurent my thanks for generous information on Antillean mollusks they too have met on their travels in the islands. To Henri Petitjean Roget my sincere thanks for his introduction to the fascinating nature of the mysteries of Arawak art; to Janine Bourveau who unhesitatingly assisted in the unattractive task of reference work, and to R. Tucker Abbott who helped in editorial matters, my deepest thanks.

39.

139. **Crassispira gibbosa** *is an active night hunter in the offshore waters of Venezuela. (1.7")*

125

Glossary of Shell Terms

Most words used in this shell book may be found in a good dictionary. The specialized terms used to describe the anatomical parts of mollusks are found in advanced identification books. The terms listed here frequently occur in shell books and have a special connotation in conchology.

aberrant form: unusual or freak shape or color.

adult form: fully grown; sexually mature.

albino form: all white in shell or soft parts.

aperture: opening or "mouth" of a snail shell.

apex: the beginning, smaller whorls in the upper (or posterior) end of a gastropod shell.

author: name of the person who described the taxonomic unit (family, genus, species or subspecies). The author's name is followed by the date of publication, e.g.: *Conus mus* Hwass, 1792.

beachworn shell: specimen of poor color and badly worn by beach conditions.

benthal: living in the ocean at depths exceeding 10,000 feet.

binomial (nomenclature): having two names, a genus and trivial (or species) name.

bivalve: member of the class Bivalvia or Pelecypoda; a clam, oyster or cockle shell.

Cenozoic: geological era extending from the Paleocene, up through the Tertiary period to, and including, the present (or Recent) epoch.

cf (confer): Sometimes put in front of a name to mean that the shell being identified is close to, but not exactly, a certain species (example: of *Conus clenchi* Martin, 1943).

conch: a large gastropod marine shell, such as a triton shell, *Strombus, Turbinella, Fasciolaria*, etc.

conchology: the study of mollusks, usually, but not necessarily, confined to the shell.

cotype: a specimen among those originally used in describing a new species, but from a series in which no holotype was selected (*syntype* is more commonly used).

crab specimen: a shell, usually in poor condition, formerly used as a home for a hermit crab. The columella may have a U-shaped worn area.

dextral form: a gastropod shell coiling clockwise (when viewed toward the apex); "right-handed".

diagnosis: short, comparative description of a species.

diameter: greatest width of a snail shell at right angles to the shell axis.

dimorphism: condition of a species having two different inherited, morphological forms, such as males being smaller or of different coloration (sexual dimorphism) than the females.

dioecious: individuals being either male or female (not hermaphrodites or monoecious, such as in the pulmonate and opisthobranch snail which have both sets of sex organs in every individual).

ecologic form: a morphological condition brought about by the influence of the environment, such as long spines in quiet waters. Also an ecotype or ecophenotypic variation.

endemic: living in a certain geographical area, and usually originally confined to that region.

fathom (fm.): six feet.

fauna: assemblage of animals living in a certain region. Flora refers to the plant life.

form or forma: a minor genetic variant, color phase, aberration, or variation due to diet or environment.

gastropod: member of the class Gastropoda, as a snail, whelk, conch, periwinkle, volute and so forth.

genotype: in nomenclature and classification this refers to the species which has been selected to be the representative type of the genus. Preferably referred to as the "Type species".

genus: a group of species seemingly closely related.

gerontic form: an oversized or worn condition due, in part, to old age.

grading system: degrees of condition of specimens usually employed by shell dealers.

> Gem: perfect quality.
> Fine +: very slightly irregular.
> Fine: minor breaks or scars.
> Good: deficient in one character, as color, otherwise fine.
> Fair: with either major break or poor color.
> Poor: badly beachworn; major breaks.

growth lines: marks or flaws in the shell due to varying rates of growth or to changing environmental conditions.

habitat: the place where a species or individual customarily lives.

hermaphrodite: an individual having the organs

of both sexes, as in all pulmonate and opisthobranch snails and some bivalves.

hinge: the upper thickened edge of the valve of a bivalve, usually with interlocking teeth and a ligament providing a hinge effect.

holotype: the specimen used in the description of a new species and selected to represent the species. The remaining specimens are paratypes.

homonym: the same name applied to two or more things or species. The later or junior homonym cannot be used and must be replaced by another name.

hybrid: offspring coming from the parents of two different populations, usually different species.

intertidal zone: seaside zone between high and low tide marks.

lot: one or more specimens of one species from one locality collected about the same time.

malacology: study of mollusks, especially the soft parts.

mantle: a skin cape that creates the shell in mollusks.

melanistic form: black or nearly black color form of a species.

monoecious: having both sexes in one individual.

monograph: an advanced and comprehensive treatment of a family or a group of species or genera.

nomen dubium: a name applied to an unrecognizable species that has an inadequate description or illustration.

ontogeny: study of the growth stages and development of an individual.

operculum: a horny or shelly "trapdoor" found in some gastropods, sometimes used to close the aperture of the shell.

paratype: after the selection of the holotype, the remaining specimens used in describing the species.

pelagic: living at the surface of the ocean, or customarily free-swimming in the ocean, such as *Janthina, Argonauta* and many squids.

periostracum: an outer, chitinous, protective layer covering the shell, sometimes smooth, rough or hairy.

phylogeny: the study of family trees or the history of the evolution of various groups of species.

phylum: a higher taxonomic group of major uniqueness, such as the starfish and sea urchins (phylum Echinodermata) or the mollusks (phylum Mollusca).

plankton: plants and animals, usually very small, that are free-swimming or floating in

polymorphic: having several different genetic forms within the same species.

polytypic species: a species having several subspecies or geographical races.

prodissoconch: embryonic shell of a bivalve or scaphopod. In gastropods called a protoconch.

radula: a tooth found on the lingual ribbon. Plural: radulae. Found in all classes of mollusks, except bivalves.

range: geographic area in which a species lives.

Recent: the present geologic epoch. The word is usually capitalized; a living species.

sculpture: the surface markings on a shell, such as ribs, scales, cords, etc.

sinistral: coiling counterclockwise, or "left-handed." When a sinistral gastropod is held with the apex up and the aperture towards the viewer, the aperture is on the left side.

species: a distinct, genetically isolated series of actually or potentially interbreeding populations.

subspecies: a geographical, somewhat isolated, race with minor differences.

substrate: the floor or bottom of the water, usually of sand, coral or rock.

syntype: one of several specimens used in an original description, formerly called a cotype.

taxon: any taxonomic unit such as a species, a subgenus, genus or family. Pleural: *taxa.*

taxonomy: the study of classification and identification.

Tertiary: geological era extending from the Paleocene to the Pleistocene (about 60 millions years duration).

topotype: specimens collected at the type locality, usually at a later time.

type: specimen(s) used in describing a new species (see holotype and paratype).

valve: one half of shell of a bivalve clam.

variety: a minor form, such as a special color or shape, but not a subspecies.

varix (pleural: *varices*): elevated, axial rib on the whorls of a snail, sometimes bladelike or frilled.

veliger: molluscan larval stage, usually free-swimming.

vernacular name: the name of a taxon in any language other than the language of zoological nomenclature. Popular or common name.

whelk: any large snail shell, usually a *Fasciolaria, Colus* or *Cittarium.*

whorl: a complete turn of a coiled snail shell.

Index

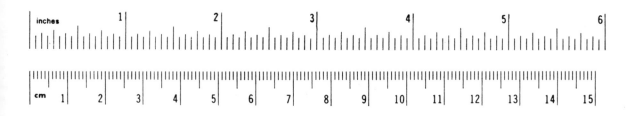